Marianne Bazzle
May, 1994

Marianne Bazzle
May, 1994

# A Place in the Country

## Country Home®

### Collection

Meredith® Books
Des Moines

# Country Home.

**Meredith® Books**
President, Book Group: Joseph J. Ward
Vice President and Editorial Director: Elizabeth P. Rice
Executive Editor: Nancy N. Green
Art Director: Ernest Shelton

**Country Home®**
Editor in Chief: Molly Culbertson
Managing Editor: Beverly Hawkins
Art Director: Peggy A. Fisher

Copy Chief/Production Editor: Angela K. Renkowski
Interior Design Director: Candace Ord Manroe
Design Editor: Joseph Boehm
Building Editor: Steve Cooper
Food and Features Editor: Lisa Kingsley
Antiques and Gardens Editor: Linda Joan Smith
Assistant Art Directors: Sue M. Ellibee, Shelley Caldwell Christy
Editorial Trainee: Michelle M. Kenyon
Administrative Assistant: Becky A. Brame
Art Business Clerk: Diana Sellers

**A PLACE IN THE COUNTRY  Country Home® Collection**
Editor in Chief: Molly Culbertson
Senior Editor: Marsha Jahns
Project Editor: Debra D. Felton
Graphic Designer: Brad Ruppert

**MEREDITH CORPORATION CORPORATE OFFICERS:**
Chairman of the Executive Committee: E.T. Meredith III
Chairman of the Board, President and
Chief Executive Officer: Jack D. Rehm
Group Presidents:
Joseph J. Ward, Books
William T. Kerr, Magazines
Philip A. Jones, Broadcasting
Allen L. Sabbag, Real Estate
**Vice Presidents:**
Leo R. Armatis, Corporate Relations
Thomas G. Fisher, General Counsel and Secretary
Larry D. Hartsook, Finance
Michael A. Sell, Treasurer
Kathleen J. Zehr, Controller and Assistant Secretary

# Contents

No matter how many homes I visit across the country, I still enjoy a sense of delight when I walk into a country house. I want to explore each corner in every room, stand still to soak in the details, hear about the home's history, and study the folk art that adorns the mantel or the quilt that graces the guest-room bed.

Because country style is so personal in its expression, its variations are limitless. That's why you'll find something new in every home we've included here. We hope this collection provides ideas, inspiration, and many hours of pleasure as you enjoy your own place in the country.

Editor in Chief

# February

## Building the Country House

# THE SUGAR

*Life can be sweet as **Country Home®** editors apply a 19th-century barn concept building a Connecticut family's dockside home.*

By Steve Cooper. Interior Design by Joseph Boehm
Produced with Ann Omvig Maine and Peggy A. Fisher

# HOUSE

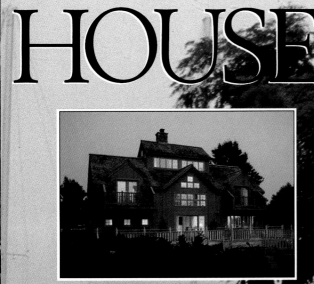

Left:
*Homeowners
Phyllis and Don
Atkinson (on far
left and right)
were assisted by
Phyllis's
daughter, Lois
Snyder, and
Rob Hyslop.*

# THE SUGAR HOUSE

*Opposite: Vivid springtime greens and pinks turn up the heat in the living room. Lois built the custom staircase, which was enhanced by the use of one-step pastel finishes on the surrounding banister woodwork.*

About a century ago, sugar houses of New England were sweet places. Still are. In small, open sheds, farm families once boiled down their harvest of maple sap—yielding a syrup rich enough to vanquish poverty itself.

By the early 19th century, smart farmers realized cramped shacks were no place to spend long, cold nights tending evaporator pans. So, they enlarged these makeshift outbuildings into sugar houses, which looked like barns except they had smaller, shedlike structures rising on their roofs to allow clouds of steam to escape.

But times change, and sugar houses, which were once built strictly for work, have been recast as playful housetop perches. As crowning, third-story rooms, they give barn-style houses an isolated escape chamber perfectly suited to leisurely pastimes, solitude, and slumber. No more boiling kettles.

"It's a perfect design for the kind of lot we have. Our house needed to go up instead of out because of . . . lot restrictions," says Phyllis Atkinson, who moved into her new high-rising home in September.

*Country Home* magazine editors joined Phyllis and her husband, Don, in creating their home overlooking a lagoon in Stamford, Connecticut. Phyllis's grown children—Lois and Bruce Snyder and Cathy Kovacs— and other friends helped address matters of style, skillful crafting, and attention to detail and color.

Like gold on an assayer's scale, the resulting home is a glowing balance of practical, everyday-living design and an ambience that is as sophisticated as it is comfortable. Notable features include the openness inherent in post-and-beam construction, freshly milled Vermont pine floors, a towering stone fireplace, bountiful expanses of glass, a kitchen designed for ease of both cooking and cleanup, a master bedroom and bathroom suite as bright as the morning, and the sugar

*Above: The living room has a cathedral ceiling open to magnificent posts and beams, but the ceiling drops low above the dining room (in background) and kitchen. Fully glazed French doors allow an unobstructed view of the lagoon.*

*Left: The apparent simplicity of a timber-frame structure is complemented by furnishings with stark lines, such as the crisp beauty of the cabinets Lois designed for both the dining room and the kitchen.*

Photographs: Bradley Olman.

Previous page: Stains, Cabot Stain Co. Opposite: Stains, Minwax Co., Inc.; floors, The Broad-Axe Beam Co.; chimney, Connecticut Stone Supply; chair and love seat, Drexel Heritage; buggy seat and round chairside table, Lineage Home Furnishings; clock sign, Ballard Designs; hardware, Baldwin Hardware from Klaff's, Inc. Top: Vertical blinds, HunterDouglas, Inc.; table and floor lamps, Tyndale, Inc.; throw, Mystic Valley Traders. Above: Tulip lamp, Lt. Moses Willard, Inc.; side chairs, Shaker Workshops

# THE SUGAR HOUSE

Above: Refrigerator and dishwasher, KitchenAid; countertop and sinks, Fountainhead by Nevamar Corp.;
laminate door inserts, Nevamar Corp.; faucets, Hansgrohe, Inc.; blinds, Duette by HunterDouglas, Inc.; Shaker oval carrier, Shaker Workshops; wood stain, Minwax

house with its daydreamer's view of the lagoon below.

The Atkinsons had decided back in 1987 to erect a 2,300-square-foot, timber-frame-style home on their coastal property. With this construction method, builders first raise a frame of thick posts and beams, then enclose the house by attaching wall panels to the outside. The frame remains visible inside the structure.

Don says, "We liked the fact that the interior spaces were so open. Also, with the posts and beams, you get a much stronger house structurally."

Purchasing a post-and-beam is different from buying a typical, contractor-built house because homeowners buy from a factory, which cuts timbers and wall panels to order. Buyers may spend months studying the sometimes subtle differences in the way companies approach construction. The Atkinsons chose the company they felt offered them the greatest flexibility in designing floor plans to suit their desires.

Left: *The same solid-surface material used for counters protects the wall around the sink.*

Above: *Gliding out on rollers, sturdy baskets are convenient storage at this bake center.*

Below: *By isolating the cooktop area, more cooks are allowed access to tools of the trade.*

Top: Oven, KitchenAid. Above: Wall clock, Shaker Workshops; radiant-heat ceiling panels, Enerjoy by Solid State Heating Corp.

# THE SUGAR HOUSE

Above: Bed, Lineage Home Furnishings; wing chair, Thomasville Furniture Industries, Inc.; fabrics,
Stroheim & Romann, Inc.; area rug, Sara Hotchkiss; lamp, Tyndale, Inc.; sheets, Wamsutta/Pacific Home Products; quilt, Appalachian House

Left: *French doors in both upstairs bedrooms open onto fresh-air balconies. This is the best spot in the house to study how beams are notched and pegged together.*

Above: *Basing her design on furniture found in a book on Shaker style, Lois made the sink vanity from cherry wood. The angles of the shower enclosure and whirlpool keep the bathroom from becoming a box. The sea-green wall was painted by Phyllis's son, Bruce Snyder, of Buffalo.*

But before hoisting the first beam, the homeowners needed to obtain construction permits. However, building in a sensitive environment raises a host of complex issues. So, the process took five years and repeated meetings with city, state, and federal agencies.

"We knew it would be a lengthy process. But we had no idea it would take so long," Phyllis says. "There were miles and miles of paperwork."

When permits were finally granted, they stipulated the family build a costly 80-foot seawall to protect their shoreline and house. The 16-foot-high block wall also had to have 100 tons of rock bolstering it.

When the lot was prepared at last, Douglas fir timbers and wall systems were delivered as a package to the lot. The basic shell was up in about two weeks. However, the finished product required six months of additional labor.

"The real work and the real costs are in the finishing," Don says. "You can't just throw up a lot of drywall and paint—you have to maneuver around those beams."

As construction progressed, the Atkinsons and *Country Home* editors sought the richest return possible on design investments. This was ensured by combining a soothing and surprising mix of colors, textures, and patterns.

The open relationships between living room, dining room, and kitchen dictated a unified color scheme. Teals and greens emerged as colors with enough vibrancy to make an impression in the expansive downstairs rooms and on the quilt-patterned floor of the master bathroom.

While most interiors with fir posts and beams are sealed with clear finishes for a natural look, a home overlooking a yacht-filled harbor requires a brush of sophistication. So, the heavy interior frame was pickled with a translucent white stain, which mutes the wood's grain without completely covering it. In the living room, this treatment softens and quiets the mood.

Above: Floor tiles, Mannington Ceramic Tiles; shower enclosure, Sterling Plumbing Group; whirlpool tub, Pearl Baths, Inc.; towels, Royal Velvet by Fieldcrest; wall-hanging fabric, Waverly/Schumacher; counter and shower walls, Fountainhead; plumbing, Pacific Plumbing Supply

# THE SUGAR HOUSE

Left: *The Atkinsons looked for a timber-frame company willing to design a third-story sugar house. Not all of them would. After looking at the plans and work of several regional builders, Don says, "Most companies in this business want to limit you to their plans. We wanted one that would build to suit our needs."*

Because the kitchen opens onto the living room, cabinets and counters became an important design element. Lois Snyder is a professional cabinetmaker, and she chose cherry wood for the project and highlighted it with door-and-island panels made from a speckled plastic laminate with a folk-art look. Lois's handiwork turned the kitchen into dessert for the eyes.

While downstairs rooms were designed with company in mind, the upper stories offer escape. The master bedroom-bathroom suite is a private haven.

But it's the third-story sugar house that gives the house its distinction. Viewed from outside, the lofty upper sanctuary towers toward the Connecticut sky, just as its simple, 19th-century predecessors did. Inside, it's a welcome chamber of complete tranquillity.

With a row of windows on each side, the sugar house is flooded with light. Where better to curl up with a book or magazine? Or gaze out at sloops lining the harbor?

Daydreaming aside, a house with so much to offer

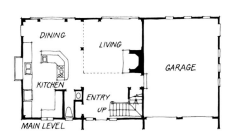

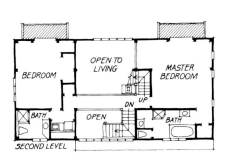

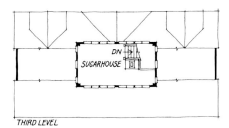

14

Floor-plan illustration by Carson Ode. Above: Settee and painted oval boxes, Shaker Workshops; chest and small painted box, Conway's Antiques and Decor; quilted pillow, The Gazebo of New York

doesn't happen without first facing a seemingly endless array of practical issues. Decisions are needed about everything from paint color to how many lights the kitchen will need. These details make the difference in creating a home with the strong character, soothing appearance, and efficiency of the Atkinsons' house.

The notable features of this house took plenty of forethought.

● Exterior colors were critical. A gray finish was chosen to give the newly constructed home a somewhat-weathered appearance.

Stain usually is applied after cedar siding is nailed in place, but extra precaution was taken here. Each plank was liberally soaked on both sides by dipping it into a stain-filled trough to increase its resistance to the elements.

● To cut costs, the Atkinsons did as much of the work themselves as they could. This included setting up 20-foot scaffolding in the living room so they could sand and finish the highest beams and the pine-plank cathedral ceiling.

● Inch-thick, shiplap pine floors were specifically cut for the Atkinsons by a Vermont mill. Each board was screwed down to ensure the boards remain flat.

● Designing the kitchen meant hiding some of its messier elements from view, says Lois, who has a bachelor's degree in woodworking.

Lois says, "I started with the basic idea that I wanted to take the meat of the kitchen—the working area—and put it out of view from those who might be in the living room. So, I raised the island and put the bake center around a corner."

She equipped the bake center with plenty of shelves for small appliances, a combination conventional/convection oven, a slide-out work surface, and roll-out, stacked wire baskets for storing spices and staples.

"The roll-outs are incredibly solid, and they help organize everything you need," says Lois. "They give the cabinetry commercial quality, though they're made for the home."

Another quality touch is the finish on the cherry-wood cabinets in the kitchen. Lois applied a one-step gel finish, which includes both the stain

# THE SUGAR HOUSE
# DETAILS

Above: *A corner of the upstairs master bedroom is a good place to view the technique used by Timberpeg, Inc., to join frames. Pieces up to 16 feet in length are mortised, tenoned, and pegged together. Typically, house frames are hidden inside walls, but with a timber-frame structure, the posts and beams go up first, then the outer walls.*

Above: *A microcomputer controls the operation of a fan high up on the living room ceiling. Long-term reliability is assured by such Casablanca Fan Co. features as a cast-metal body, baked enamel finish, and a motor with precision-sealed bearings. Not only does it look good, but it also will help keep the house cooler in summer and warmer in winter.*

Above: *The laundry center was placed between the two upstairs bedrooms. A Whirlpool Corp. washer/dryer unit saves space, but doesn't skimp on capacity. The Sterling Plumbing Group faucet has a single-handle control and a pull-out spray.*

and a durable, polyurethane topcoat.

● In the bathroom, Lois adapted the design of a Shaker kitchen worktable for her cherry sink vanity. She also made the matching mirror surround and decorative Shaker peg rail for towels. To build everything, Lois turned the Atkinsons' garage into a shop and recruited a friend, Rob Hyslop, to assist.

"Though the shop was cramped, there's an advantage in working right at the site rather than from a set of plans," Lois says. "I was able to make sure everything fits proportionally into spaces."

● To create a seascape wall in the bathroom, Bruce Snyder put on four coats of green latex paint. The secret, he says, is to work quickly.

"If you use a high-quality latex, the trick is that the paint will start drying as soon as you put it on. So you have to work fast," Bruce says.

First, he rolled on a coat of dark green and let it dry. Then, he rolled on a second coat of dark green. Before this coat could dry, he began applying medium and light shades of green paint.

"I used a crinkly plastic bag from a grocery store to put on those last coats," Bruce says. "I'd go back and forth between the paints, putting on one shade and then the other. You sort of swirl it on. This has to be done while the undercoat is still wet to get a liquid look."

He recommends using a semigloss paint. A glossy paint can reflect light in odd, unappealing ways.

● The pattern seen on the tile floor of the bathroom was inspired by an old quilt. The floor was adapted by Melanie Wood, a designer for Mannington Ceramic Tile.

● The Atkinsons chose radiant heat to warm the house. The energy-efficient system uses lightweight, inch-thick electric panels mounted on the ceiling to heat without ducts, fans, or sound.

The panels emit a sunlike heat that is absorbed into furnishings. As objects in the room release their heat, the room gets warmer.

With all this planning and detail—from exterior colors to the heating system—the Atkinsons tapped into value, quality, and craftsmanship. Life is sweet indeed. □

# THE SUGAR HOUSE
# DETAILS

*Left: Taking the sea as his inspiration, Bruce Snyder created a swirling, fluid look for the wall next to the whirlpool tub. With Benjamin Moore semigloss latex paints, he rolled on two coats of dark green. Then, using a crinkled plastic bag, he added two more coats of medium green and light green.*

Above: *Those small black boxes on each of the Andersen Windows, Inc., windows are the company's electric openers, which replace the usual long, inconvenient cranks. With the flip of a single switch, a whole row of out-of-reach windows will open. There are also rain sensors telling the system when it is time to tightly close.*

Above: *Hafele America Co.'s durable accessories, such as this fold-out, pantry basket system, make it easier to find what you need in a hurry. Phyllis's daughter, Cathy Kovacs, painted the vine pattern around the window.*

# TIME'S HIDDEN
# *Treasure*

**WITH A HUNCH AND A GOOD EYE, THE KIMBLES
FOUND THEIR ANTIQUE VERMONT HOME BURIED BENEATH
LAYERS OF AGE AND ADDITIONS.**

Twenty years of living in Vermont, plus backgrounds in art and antiques, equipped Warren and Lorraine Kimble with their fair share, and then some, of Yankee ingenuity. Particularly when it came to houses. They had restored no fewer than 11 historic homes, so they well knew the difference between those architectural features that constituted character and those that amounted to no more than clutter.

They also knew that, beneath the clutter, might rest a gem.

**BY CANDACE ORD MANROE**

Photographs: William N. Hopkins, Hopkins Associates.

# Treasure

Above: *Warren and Lorraine Kimble enjoy the sun on the patio just outside Warren's studio at the rear of their home.*

Bottom right: *The front entry features a carving of Lincoln by 25-year-old folk artist Chris LaMontagne of Rhode Island; Lorraine stenciled the floors.*

Left: *In the living room, an old tavern tabletop with breadboard ends serves as a cocktail table, adding a homespun country air to the more formal mood set by a pair of wing chairs ("semi-antiques," according to Warren).*

Top: *A highly stylized Holstein painted by Warren is a best-selling print among his fans.*

That's exactly what they found in Brandon, a west-central Vermont town skirted with rolling green meadows, classic red dairy barns, and centuries-old clapboard farmhouses.

"The house was covered in bland gray, man-made siding from the 1930s and '40s," says Warren, a folk artist and former college art teacher. "But we saw beyond that."

"We noticed the dentil molding and front door," adds Lorraine, who helps run an art gallery in nearby Rutland. "These were our clues to the fact that this house was more than it appeared to be."

It was, indeed, more. The house Warren and Lorraine purchased and lovingly restored five years ago was older than it looked: It dates to the early 1800s. It also had more charm than anyone but the Kimbles had anticipated.

Once they peeled off the siding to reveal original clapboards painted yellow ochre and removed a front sun porch to restore the facade to its original Federal style, that charm began peeking through.

"We kept the original ochre paint on the exterior and stained over it, creating a slightly darker color," says Warren, "but as the stain ages, a beautiful golden hue that's very subtle shows through from the original paint." Similarly, the original milk-based red paint on the dentil moldings declares itself

# Treasure

from beneath a top coat, creating a luminous yet still mellow color.

After ridding the home of extraneous features that had been added over the years, the Kimbles still had more work to do before turning their attention to decorating the interior. A new foundation was needed on three sides of the house. The rotted windows required replacement, along with many of the walls. A second bathroom was needed, as well as heating.

Throughout the restoration process—which, amazingly, took only three months—the couple

stuck close to the original design of the house. Even seemingly unglamorous features such as the woodshed at the back were salvaged. With a little help, that space now serves as Warren's imminently sunny studio, while the loft above it—once used for raising baby turkeys—now is the airy, spacious master bedroom.

Once original features were uncovered, the Kimbles set about bringing those elements back into prominence. Overall, they were lucky: Much of the early structure remained intact, including the pine floorboards and downstairs ceiling beams,

Right: *In the dining room, a circa-1840 worktable is decorated with new folk art and flanked by painted step-down Windsors. Warren carved the heron by the window as an anniversary present for Lorraine.*

Bottom left: *Warren embellished an antique Pennsylvania jelly cupboard with murals. He also made the Noah's ark, then he collected various artists' animals, two at a time.*

Top: Checkerboard Cats *is another popular painting of Warren's available in prints.*

*Left: Warren and
Lorraine retrieved an
old store counter from
Shapiro's department
store in Brandon when
the building was
remodeled. They
transformed it into a
kitchen island cook
surface, outfitting it
with a stove, as well as
West Rutland,
Vermont, marble
inserts for preparing
dough. Warren created
a mural effect on the
counter, painting tree-
shaded scenes within
each of the side panels.*

*Right: The gardens are
proof of another of
Lorraine's talents.*

*Top: Warren's art
decorates tiny boxes.*

# Treasure

all of which the Kimbles promptly exposed. "All we had to do to the ceiling beams was apply a stain to even out the color," says Warren.

Then they put their real artistic talents to work to enhance the structure, as well as the furnishings within it. The floors became Lorraine's responsibility. In the mudroom, which is so well-designed as to be almost a misnomer, she hand-cut and laid slate roofing material into a mosaic-patterned slate floor. "I had never done anything like this before, but figured if other people could, I could, too," explains Lorraine.

Her "I can-do-it" attitude resulted in other beautiful floors, which feature her handiwork with decorative paint techniques. In the upstairs bathroom (the

only bath original to the home), she sponged the floor green, then combed it around the room's perimeter to create a fanciful border. Lorraine used a combination of three different decorative paint treatments— combing, sponging, and stenciling—to make the floor the pièce de résistance in an upstairs bedroom.

Lorraine's talents with paint are evident upon entering the home: She stenciled the entry's floor in a bold red-and-white checkerboard pattern.

While Lorraine's artistic abilities are geared toward the functional (you can, after all, walk on her beautifully painted floors), Warren's are intended for aesthetic appreciation only. By the time he and Lorraine bought the house, he had left

# Treasure

academia to pursue his own art. In harmony with the character of the Kimbles' newly acquired historic digs, that art had become simpler and more whimsical both in subject matter and in style, evolving into the stylized folk art that's easily identifiable as his own.

Once they were living in the house, Warren not only was able to paint his favorite folk art themes—Holstein cows, cats, antique houses, and Noah's ark creatures—for sale to the public, but he also was able to embellish certain furnishings in the home with painted scenes, just for Lorraine's and his pleasure. For example, on the kitchen island, which had been a display counter in a Brandon

department store, he painted scenes within the side panels.

Warren is no prima donna when it comes to his folk art: He actively collects works by other artists, as a quick glance about his home proves—starting with the Abe Lincoln carving that stands sentry at the front door.

Antique American country furnishings complement the home's folk art and its age. Longtime collectors and dealers, the Kimbles furnished the home in pieces from the early 1800s, adding to the home's period authenticity. Having delivered a treasure from the not-so-gentle hands of time, Warren and Lorraine are capable stewards, treating their find with care, always respecting its integrity. □

Right: *This guest bedroom bespeaks serenity with its calm colors and selective accessories: a circa-1850 coverlet, a sampler signed and dated in 1842, a new folk-art crow, and Christmas sheep from the 1920s.*

Bottom left: *Another room features a lift-top blanket chest and painted boxes, (both c. 1830) and an arrow-back rocker (c. 1840).*

Above: *Lorraine sponged and combed the bathroom floor.*

Top left: *The hare is another folk theme stylized by Warren.*

# Masterworks from the MOUNTAIN

*Her talents tested by a growing season that's short but sweet, gardener Suzy McCleary grows a palette of brilliant blooms high in the Colorado Rockies.*

Like the wild larkspur that blooms briefly above the timberline, Suzy McCleary's garden is a surprising thing. Overshadowed by the barren peaks of the Rocky Mountains, the garden is an ephemeral Eden, thriving in spite of the harsh alpine weather. Some years, winter maintains its icy grip on the land well into June, then the first fall frost descends at Labor Day. Yet, for a few short weeks in July and August, this sheltered mountain acreage comes alive with color, providing Suzy—an artist with flowers—with all the materials she needs for her bountiful bouquets.

During summer, as plants mature and blossoms unfold, Suzy composes floral still lifes for hotels, homes, and weddings, all the while drying an abundance of flowers and herbs for use during the winter. Both a pleasure and a livelihood, the flower and herb business—called Clear Water Farm—grew out of her passion for mountain solitude, a longtime love of

**By Mindy Pantiel and Linda Joan Smith**

❦

**Opposite:** *Old-time favorites—delphinium, sweet pea, columbine, yarrow, and cosmos—are mixed masterfully in this lush bouquet.*

**Left:** *Raised in Yosemite, Suzy McCleary thrives in the Rocky Mountain valley she calls home.*

**Below:** *During the summer, the McClearys' cottage is embraced by blooms; near Christmas it becomes a showcase for Suzy's dried flowers.*

gardening, and her education in fine art.

Suzy uses her flower beds as a painter does a palette. "I love to mix all kinds of things together and try different color combinations," she says. Because of their many blooms, Suzy prefers annuals, and plants as many as 50 types. Statice, baby's breath, larkspur, and cosmos are favorites.

Cultivated flowers form the heart of her arrangements, but Suzy's bouquets have a hint of wildness to them that has become a signature of sorts. She often twines wild vines around the flowers, their tendrils trailing to the tabletop, and she laces in whatever else she finds on her mountain forays, from chokecherry blossoms to small branches of red twig dogwood.

Suzy's affinity for wild plants was cultivated during her childhood years, spent in Yosemite National Park where her father worked. "For the first part of my life, I never knew there was such a thing as a nursery," she says. "My mother had beautiful gardens, and she was always collecting seeds from her favorite wild plants and growing them in our yard."

With late springs and early frosts, Suzy has only a few brief months to bring her garden from seed into full flower. To get the jump on Mother Nature, she starts most of her plants in the greenhouse in early March, then transplants them into earth enriched with "old manure by the truck load."

"The growing season is so short here some people think you're crazy to try," she says. "It's harder, but the blooms are more vivid and beautiful than any I've ever seen."

There are other rewards to the brief growing season. There's time, during the winter months, to transform bundles of dried flowers—from stock to love-in-a-mist—into wreaths and other colorful arrangements. There's time to make hundreds of bars of herbal-scented soap: calendula lavender, oatmeal sage, and peppermint aloe vera. And there's time for Suzy and her husband, Paul, to hold their eagerly awaited, annual Christmas bazaar, for which they fill the rooms of their tiny cottage with dried arrangements, jars of homemade jam, their soaps, and other locally made wares.

Most of all, as snow blankets the fields and calls a halt to summer's labors, there's time to plan, to sketch out new garden plots, to order new seeds to try, and to dream of yet another artful harvest. □

❧

**Opposite:** *Flowers dried during the brief summer growing season keep Suzy supplied with materials throughout the winter months.*

**Left:** *Bouquets, wreaths, and bundles of dried flowers express Suzy's artistic side and often contain unexpected touches of dried citrus slices and wild seed pods.*

**Below:** *Suzy's gardens—more than a dozen of them—are set in niches carved into the forest on the 5-acre property.*

*A lush oasis in the middle of the New Mexico desert, Tesuque offers the best of both worlds for Jane Smith and Craig Huitfeldt.*

# ABUNDANCE ON THE ARROYO

As much as they love the Southwest's hardscrabble swells of sagebrush and piñon, where the dry air blows even drier with caliche dust, Jane Smith and her husband, Craig Huitfeldt, are shade-tree-and-water folks at heart. So, as newlyweds ready to set up housekeeping in New Mexico—a state mythologized for its badlands and bleached bones (thanks, in large part, to Georgia O'Keefe)—they seriously considered only one place: Tesuque.

Located on the Old Taos Highway about 5 miles north of Santa Fe and 70 miles south of Taos, Tesuque is a geographical anomaly. Shouldered between the rough, red-baked ridges of the desert, it is a hidden valley cut by the cool waters of an arroyo and canopied by the wide branches of tall trees.

"I lived in Tesuque for two years before I met

**BY CANDACE ORD MANROE
PRODUCED BY NANCY INGRAM**

**Above:** *Jane Smith and Craig Huitfeldt find their brick-paved portal ideal for relaxing in Mexican chairs.* **Left and bottom left:** *Landscaping was central to the redo.* **Far left and top:** *Native American artifacts and cowboy collectibles in the living room express regional style.*

Photographs: Gene Johnson.

31

**Right:** *The living room includes a custom cowboy lamp with rawhide shade and an old Taos Indian drum as a table base.*

**Far right:** *Stucco walls, whitewashed pine floors, and cathedral ceilings with split, hand-hewn vigas showcase the living room's Southwestern furnishings.*
**Above:** *Spanish antiques set the home's mood in the entry hall.*

Craig, and I really loved the setting and privacy of the small village," remembers Jane. "When Craig and I married four years ago and decided to buy a home, I said, 'It's got to be in Tesuque.'"

There, three years ago, they found the perfect property. Willowy aspens fluttered in the breeze, joining other deciduous trees in hemming the grounds with a sense of seclusion—a considerable feat in a region of expansive vistas and bustling tourism.

But, unfortunately, this perfect property did *not*

contain the perfect house. Entirely too cramped at only 800 square feet, the existing home featured a pint-size kitchen and a combined living and dining area that also included a bedroom alcove. Still, the couple saw potential—a *lot* of potential.

After a year in limbo waiting for the owners to accept their offer, Jane and Craig got to work, more than tripling the size of the house to 2,900 square feet, overhauling the original portion, and extensively landscaping the grounds. Craig, who works as a real estate developer, designed the new floor plan, and Jane, a sweater designer with shops in Santa Fe and Aspen, put her discerning eye to work decorating the home's interiors.

The couple took their design cues from the original adobe structure, which was built in the territorial style—one of the region's two types of indigenous architecture (the other is pueblo). Territorial design was born when the railroad ventured West, bringing in its wake a pastiche of Eastern building styles that merged with the Southwest's pueblo tradition, blending adobe exteriors with elements of California mission, Greek Revival, Mediterranean, and Victorian. Unlike

## ABUNDANCE ON THE ARROYO

Left: *Family cowboy boots decorate the brick window ledge overlooking the side patio. (Brick is used around all windows in the home.)*

pueblo style, which is noted for its curving, sculptural forms, territorial design is linear and sharp-angled, more geometric than fluid.

In the Tesuque home, the style translated as a tin, pitched roof, as opposed to the flat pueblo, and to rectangular, rather than arched, doorways.

"It was beautiful to watch the craftsmen build this house," says Jane. "Everybody involved seemed to be an artisan and took such pride in their work. In fact, we had a party for all the craftsmen when the house was completed. It was wonderful watching all the elements of the house come together."

In their redo, the couple made sure the portal leading into the house actually became an outdoor extension of the home's living space. It serves as a peaceful veranda for relaxing and enjoying the gentle, soft-focus New Mexico dawns and the more intense, fiery sunsets—always to the mellifluous music of the Little Tesuque River.

To complete the property's oasis ambience, Craig took responsibility for the landscaping. He spared the existing trees, then transformed the plain grounds into a verdant, lively garden. And, much to skeptical Jane's

surprised delight, his efforts reached fruition only a scant year later.

"The landscaping really was the icing on the cake," says Jane. Craig adds, "It ties the whole house together as it winds its way around the house. The flagstone patios and paths define the parameters of the house."

Like Craig's territorial-style architecture, Jane's interior design reflects the blend of influences that merged during the frontier days of westward expansion via railroad. The home's crisp-lined, white stucco rooms, with

Far left: *An elk head presides over the dining room, which includes an antique pine table and leather Mexican chairs. The pine lintel above the French doors features hand-carved bluebirds.*
Above: *A horn chandelier is the kitchen's focal point.*

echoes, in some way, of the essence and fiber of the Southwest—imbue the home with much more than one-of-a-kind character. With every decorating and building material having its own story, the home seems almost a personal museum of Southwestern craft.

The upstairs main living spaces are a melange of decorative elements, from a contemporary sofa and wrought-iron cocktail table in the living room to the Navaho rug and Spanish-influenced table and chairs in the dining room. But the downstairs guest quarters are what Jane calls "pure cowboy." The bedroom, den, and adjoining bath pay homage to the Old West, with furnishings and accessories reminiscent of the "cowboy kitsch" one still might encounter today at a dude ranch cabin or lodge.

Throughout the home, a number of New Mexico antiques are mixed with Western and Native American handcrafted pieces, giving the home a warm, timeless quality.

Having found their lush enclave, Craig and Jane never forget that its context is pure desert: Mounted above their doorways, bleached skulls like those in an O'Keefe painting are reminders that New Mexico is, after all, the badlands. □

**Right** *and* **top:** *True 1950s' cowboy spirit reigns in the lower-level guest suite, with wagon-wheel furniture, calfskin on the sofa, a Navaho ladder with old Pendleton blankets and Indian rugs, and a handmade cowboy bed and spread.* **Above:** *A huge cedar bed graces this room.*

their hand-hewn vigas supporting cathedral ceilings, are filled with an eclectic mix of historic Native American artifacts and contemporary cowboy collectibles. Together, the elements make a strong regional style statement.

Furnishings and accessories, like the structure itself, are, for the most part, handcrafted. Hand-carved furniture and sculpture, handwoven Native American baskets, rugs, and pillows, wrought-iron accessories, and handcrafted lamps—all

# Shared Vision

**Beth and Barry Smiley didn't always see eye to eye on the country life they now cherish at their farmhouse in eastern Iowa.**

Between bites of chocolate doughnuts and cups of fresh coffee served at the Midwestern restaurant where she worked, Beth Smiley first envisioned life with her favorite customer, Barry. Little in their personal histories foreshadowed the idyllic setting in which the couple lives today: a restored 1860s farmhouse filled with antiques, skirted by a white picket fence, and drenched in the shade of a dozen walnut trees.

At the time, Beth could hardly see beyond the shiny sports car Barry pulled into the Dunkin' Donuts parking lot in each morning on his way home from work as a firefighter.

"Some of the firemen would come into the shop after they got off work at seven. That's how we met," says Beth, who now works as a substitute school teacher. "Barry had a canary yellow Corvette, and I was really into Corvettes. I almost had enough money saved up to buy one when I met him."

Beth never got her own Corvette, but she did win Barry's affections. The two were married in 1979.

"When I met Barry, he lived in a little apartment where everything was chrome and glass," Beth

**BY BEVERLY HAWKINS
PRODUCED WITH SUE MATTES**

❧

Left *and* below: *Most of the work Beth and Barry Smiley,* above, *completed on their stone farmhouse in eastern Iowa restored the structure to its original 1860s form. The couple took creative license, however, on the surrounding grounds. Barry added the picket fence and arbor, and dug the garden pond within view of the barn that houses his workshop and an upstairs apartment for his grown son Rob. "I think Barry dug the pond three or four times before he finally got it just right," Beth says. They then landscaped around the pond, laid brick sidewalks, and built a garden bench.*

# Shared Vision

remembers. One of his prized possessions was a framed 8×10-inch piece of celluloid from the Walt Disney animated movie *Robin Hood.* In those days, antiques were objects of scorn to Barry, who often chided his brother for collecting what he called "old junk."

It was Beth who, despite a love for flashy cars, introduced Barry to the beauty of old pine and painted pieces. After their marriage, she convinced him to take a vacation to Colonial Williamsburg, Virginia, one of the largest living history museums in the world. There they fell in love with the look and feel of colonial America.

"We started dreaming of owning a stone house with

land and a place for a workshop," Beth says. "We wanted to find an old farmhouse that wasn't in the middle of the boonies."

The couple was living in a small bungalow that Barry remodeled using his skills as a carpenter—a job he held before joining the fire department and one he returned to after retiring in 1981. When the remodeling was complete, and Barry found himself starting over on the house, the couple knew it was time to find a new home.

Unexpectedly, they came across a two-bedroom farmhouse that was set on 3 acres not far from the heart of a nearby Mississippi River town. The stone house was built in 1860 by a machinist

❧

*Right: The Smileys purchased the mammy's bench and*
*pine chest in the living room at antiques shows in the Midwest.*
*Above: Despite choosing red trim for the main floor, Beth*
*says she and Barry are really "blue people."*

# Shared Vision

who emigrated from Germany. His wife died 10 years later, leaving him to raise three children, two of whom never married or moved from home. His last child died there in 1971 at the age of 101.

Twelve years later, Barry and Beth saw an ad for the house. "I stopped by with my daughter," says Barry, who has three sons and a daughter from a previous marriage. "As soon as I saw the house, yard, and barn, I knew it was exactly what we had been dreaming of. I said, 'We'll buy it.' We didn't even look inside."

Had he peeked beyond the front door, Barry would have discovered the outdated results of a 1970s remodeling project: a wrought-iron staircase, foil wallpaper, cork-covered kitchen walls, and glass shelving. Recent owners also had added modern plumbing and a two-story frame addition.

It was the Smileys, however, who peeled back the layers of time to highlight the home's vintage features, such as wavy glass windows and handwrought hardware.

Barry, with help from sons Rob and Tim, redid the addition in keeping with the old house's style. They replaced an iron staircase with a wooden one that is a replica of the front steps in the stone part of the old house. They replastered the kitchen, rebuilt the cabinets, and added a wood stove.

Throughout the house, windows, doors, and walls

Right: *Barry designed and built this kitchen table and bench (at left of table) based on antiques he saw at a show.* Above: *Beth's flower and herb beds flourish in the backyard where former owners once burned trash.*

## Shared Vision

were refurbished, and a screened porch with a garden view was added.

Beth directed the interior design, choosing white walls with red trim on the main floor and blue trim for the bedrooms. Her handwoven blankets, samplers, and dried flowers from the garden decorate many of the rooms.

In a stone barn that once sheltered livestock, the couple discovered a cache of antique lumber and plenty of space to build a workshop. Upstairs, Rob created an apartment

where he now lives. A clapboard addition to the barn—actually an outbuilding moved there 90 years ago when the street was put in—houses the couple's cars, including Barry's yellow Corvette.

Although they've spent the last decade shaping the home of their dreams, Beth and Barry have learned that the mind's eye is forever wandering.

"Your tastes change," Beth says. "I wouldn't do this house the same way twice. Sometimes I want to start all over again." □

---

Above: *Furnishing the bedroom was a team effort. Barry built the pencil-post bed after Beth winced at the cost of purchasing one. She wove the blanket on the chest.*

Left: *The spare bedroom reveals the home's original stone walls.*

# April

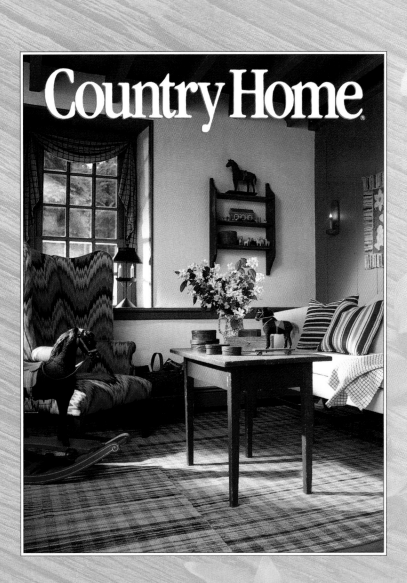

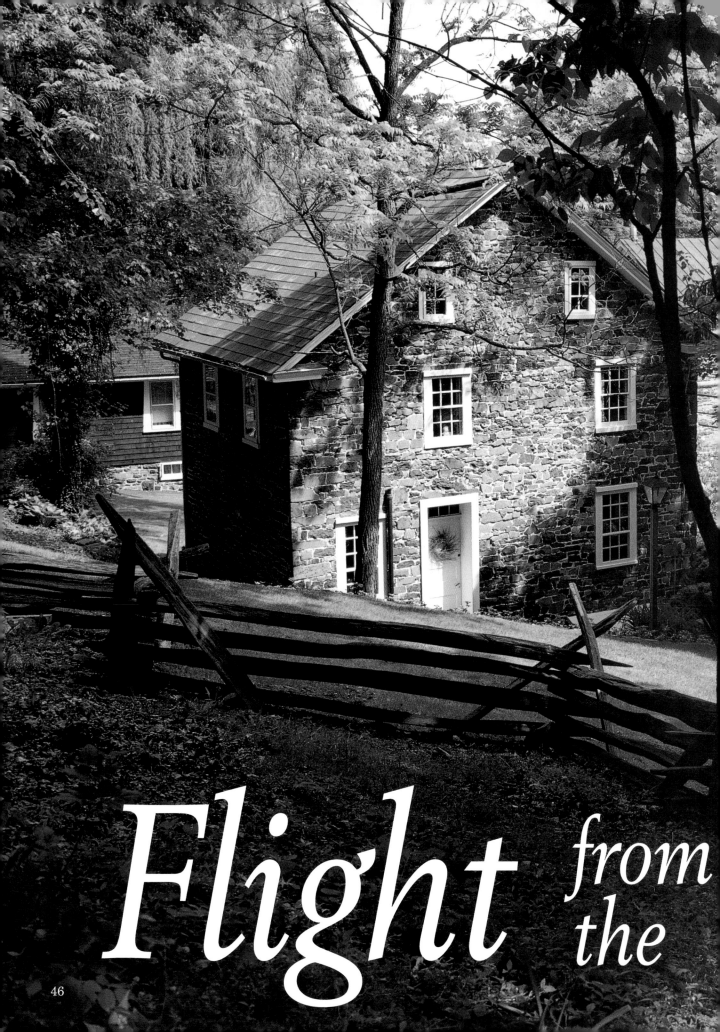

*Flight* *from the*

# City

*Though their airline careers are flying high, Kathy
and Ken Wilson always look forward to a
smooth landing back home at their 1819 stone house.*

BY ROSEMARY RENNICKE. PRODUCED BY ANN OMVIG MAINE

# Flight from the City

In this fast-paced, rush-around world, perhaps few couples are more jet-propelled than Kathy and Ken Wilson. Kathy is a flight attendant who shuttles between New York and Tokyo, and Ken manages ground operations for an airline at New Jersey's Newark Airport. Is it any wonder, then, that the two escape to the Pennsylvania hamlet of Point Pleasant, where a little stone house on the banks of a river offers them a haven?

"This is our refuge," says Ken, "a place of peace and complete tranquillity."

Career demands prompted the Wilsons' move here several years ago from the Midwest. They brought with them a long-established love for simple, Eastern-style country furnishings.

"The house we had in Minnesota was filled with antiques from across Pennsylvania and New England," Kathy says. All they lacked was the proper old house to set them off. They found it in Bucks County: a sweet, six-room shoebox of a house.

Overlooking the broad,

Top: *For fireside meals, Kathy and Ken Wilson may use the tavern table or the spacious chair-table.*
Above: *Old boxwood shrubs and rhododendrons ring the house.*
Right: *A camelback sofa and chairs with outsize wings were chosen to soften the living room's boxy dimensions.*

Photographs: William Simone and Art Clagett

# Flight from the City

rolling Delaware River, the fieldstone structure was built in 1819 by a son of the local fishery owner. The house had been expertly restored before the Wilsons bought it in 1989. Ken says, "Other houses we'd seen had been over-renovated. But here, we really felt as if we'd walked back into history."

Making that illusion real is the fact that all the beams, the back-to-back fireplaces, and much of the pine flooring were original. Restored sections—the windows and paneling, for instance—had been undertaken with appropriate materials salvaged from period houses. Electric lighting was carefully hidden in the rafters, and other modern necessities, such as heating and plumbing, were unobtrusively tucked away.

While the Wilson house is not large—indeed, it is so compact that much of the furniture for the upper floors had to be hoisted in through the second-story windows—its comforts are immeasurable. The mix of

*Top: Game boards, a set of primitive side chairs, and a curvaceous, tin candelabra brighten the kitchen.*
*Above: Casual meals are served on a battened, pig-shaped tray.*
*Right: Instead of built-in cabinets, the Wilsons prefer this freestanding mustard cupboard lined with pantry boxes.*

# Flight from the City

seamless painted antique pieces, quality reproductions, and homemade furniture creates a winsome, truly relaxing feeling. "Our lives are so busy now," says Kathy, "that we really enjoy staying home. We just like to sit in the living room and catch up on each other's day."

Painted furniture, including cupboards, blanket chests, and rope beds in warm, time-worn colors, was the starting point and remains the mainstay of the Wilsons' collection. The couple was initially drawn to the economical lines and sometimes eccentric craftsmanship of such handmade pieces. After

more than 10 years of hunting, learning, and buying, the Wilsons find that their furniture has not lost a whit of its charm. Says Ken, "I still look at the pieces and try to imagine what life was like back then and how

Top: *Putz sheep made in Germany are among the Wilsons'*
*favorites. Another prize is the small Shaker box topping the stack*
*on the upper shelf. A gift from Kathy's sister, it is dated 1770.*
Above: *A rope bed wears a piece of antique blue homespun.*
Left: *Kathy says her two Amish dolls look like sisters.*

53

# Flight from the City

her self-taught talents to their home by painting Father Christmases, Noah's arks, and other folk art figurines. She has sewn curtains and pillow covers, using either old blankets and ticking or new homespun, and has worked out perfect placement for accessories.

The Wilsons' concern for details is rooted in the pride they share in their home. At every point, the dwelling is a refreshing, bright, and joyous escape from hectic careers.

"We both grew up in small towns with simple values," says Kathy. "Maybe that's why we enjoy simple things." □

*Rosemary Rennicke is a free-lance writer from Doylestown, Pennsylvania.*

the pieces were made and used. I can see someone years ago working with their hands and old tools."

When a violent storm felled an old tree in the yard two summers ago, Ken claimed kinship to those crafters of old and built rustic furniture for the family room.

Kathy also has added

Top: *Among the pieces Ken has crafted are the rustic table and sofa seen in the third-floor family room.*
Above: *The miniature cabin is the work of a contemporary artist.*
Right: *The family room is a private retreat filled with cozy cotton Indian blankets, a rocking horse, and snowshoes.*

# EXPANDING HORIZONS

*A horticultural adventurer at heart,
Judith Gries explores a new garden territory
with each planting season.*

By Linda Joan Smith

Like ripples that radiate from a single splash in a placid pond, Judith Gries's Connecticut garden has spread ever outward from its original heart. Though the garden began just six years ago with a single riotous bed of perennials, its paths now meander among a circular bed of herbs, a multitextured display of decorative grasses, and a lushly planted "streambed," then down a formal allée (or alley) of pear trees. This year's expansion

**Far left:** *Soft blooms of roses, larkspur, yarrow, nepeta, and snapdragons fill this circular bed.*

**Left:** *Judith Gries began gardening 15 years ago and is now a master of the art.*

**Above:** *The garden embraces the back of Robert and Judith Gries's home, which began life in 1801 as the first building of the Woodstock Academy high school.*

Photographs: Judith Watts

**Above:** *A second-story window affords a grand view of some of Judith's perennial beds and the field and woods beyond. Each new bed* "follows the lay of the land," Judith says. "The setting and buildings have dictated naturally where the gardens should be."

**Far left:** *Fresh-picked flowers are one of Judith's summertime rewards. This gathering includes Queen-Anne's-lace, snapdragons,*

# EXPANDING HORIZONS

Below: *The mature growth of Judith's oldest perennial border fills one side of the yard with lush greenery and floral color from spring through fall. Brightest during July are rust-red daylilies, Japanese iris,*

*rudbeckia daisies, lady's-mantle, bee balm, zinnias, yarrow, lilies, and lysimachia—all neatly tucked into a copper tub.*

will bring more delights: a "wild" garden, lush with native flowers and shrubbery.

For Judith, each new garden area is a horticultural adventure, prompted by her reading of gardening classics and her own vivid vision and passion for experiment. Sometimes it's the only way she can incorporate a newly discovered specimen. "I fall in love with a plant I've seen, and then I've got to fit it into the garden someplace," Judith says.

Designing the new planting beds is her favorite part of gardening, but she rarely plots anything on paper. As each bed progresses and matures, she shifts plants around according to texture, height, color, and season of bloom. "I move plants

*pink and yellow oriental lilies, pink hollyhock mallow, spikes of veronica, and lacy cleome. Other plant types, such as smokebush, enkianthus, and Helen's flower, have their show later in the year.*

*Left: Gracefully arching fruit trees, sentinel-like yews, and a white lattice pergola frame the passage to the rear-most part of the garden, where graceful statuary catches the eye. Robert Gries built the fanciful pergola, which was designed by a friend.*

# EXPANDING
# HORIZONS

Opposite: *Chosen for their foliage, plants such as sedum, santolina, miscanthus, carex, and a collection of ligularia hug the banks of Judith's streambed. The rocks are a well-traveled bunch; Robert and*

like other people move furniture," she says. "People shouldn't be afraid to do that. That's how you learn."

Always one for sharing, whether plant cuttings or gardening tips, Judith has recently begun a new venture, providing other gardeners with the elements that make her own colorful beds work so well: garden ornaments, old roses, decorative grasses, and other favorite plants. Most of all, Judith hopes to share the rewards that come from working closely with the earth.

"People are always welcome to come see the garden," she says. "When I'm out there, I can forget everything else and feel totally joyful. It's my nirvana. I want other people to experience that, too." □

*Judith have brought them home from places as far flung as Nova Scotia, Cape Cod, and California's Death Valley.*

Above: *A shaded wall of shrubbery shields the oldest section of the garden from the street, providing a cool summer alcove.*

Left: *An aggregation of grasses—fountain grass, miscanthus, blood grass, and others—forms a dramatic year-round display with the bee balm and yew. "They make beautiful sculptures in the snow," says Judith.*

# CINDERELLA STORY

With a magical stroke of faux-finish artistry, Anne Klapfish transformed a Boston-area carriage house from neglected stepchild into a fantasy home her entire family can enjoy.

When Anne and her husband, Maurice, bought the circa-1860 carriage house 19 years ago—just a year after their marriage—it literally was down-at-the-heels: The kitchen floorboards had completely rotted out, leaving virtually no walking surface. Renovation work that had been com-

*Inspired by her own lawn, Anne Klapfish paints flower pots at home to sell in her shop.*

pleted by the previous owners involved large amounts of inexpensive paneling, which was not exactly the look the Klapfishes

*An admirer of FDR's Campobello, Anne reversed its colors for her home.*

had in mind for their dream home in Brookline, a manicured suburb of Boston.

"We spent a long time getting back to plaster," Anne says, keenly aware of her own understatement.

Though painstakingly implemented, almost all of the improvements the Klapfishes made were cosmetic. Only one structural change was required. "Someone had put in dreadful curlicue

BY CANDACE ORD MANROE
PRODUCED BY ESTELLE BOND GURALNICK

Right: *Anne's creative handiwork is seen in the entry hall on the faux-marble floor and stenciled wall.*
Left: *A seaside ambience pervades in the white-on-white bedroom.*

# CINDERELLA STORY

wrought-iron supports," Anne recalls, "which we replaced with wood posts."

Immediately after purchasing the carriage house, the couple agreed that it needed to be lightened and brightened. The parquet flooring and wainscoting, stained a dark shade in 1910 when the building was converted from a carriage house to a home, was too oppressive. Anne and Maurice stripped the wood back to its natural oak finish, establishing the airy environment that would characterize their subsequent decorating.

With a college background in art (and English), Anne was eager to employ her talents with paint to improve the house. Maurice, an MIT graduate and vice president of a marketing company that consults in the electronics industry, was comfortable in the role of consultant in the home decorating effort as well. He was only too happy to have Anne's creativity personalize and enliven their home.

Anne's artistry is evident upon entering the house. The entry hall floors, painted to resemble marble tiles, demonstrate

Left: *With a wreath and garland of silk ivy and roses, Anne softened the living room's ornate, mirrored mantel, installed when the carriage house was changed to a home in 1910. Floral chintz and vintage pieces, including a $100 flea market hutch, create a cheery, cottage mood.*
Above: *A 50-cent lamp becomes art with a shade Anne customized using paint, decoupage, and silk flowers.*
Top: *Anne's self-portrait hanging in a hallway was completed as an art class assignment in college.*

# CINDERELLA STORY

her proficiency as a faux-finish artist. After painting one of the entry's walls a charcoal gray, Anne added romantic flourish by stenciling cherubs, swags, and an urn upon the neutral background, using stencils she had purchased in England.

The entry also exhibits the eclectic flair—and

whimsical light touch—the owners favor throughout the home. Decked in a fresh coat of white paint, a $10 yard-sale table becomes the charming host to a collection of early-1900s plates, as well as a grouping of papier-mâché boxes from London. That ability to transform the most unlikely spaces and ordinary, inexpensive objects into strong style statements is what Anne's design skills are all about.

Real sticklers for detail and thoroughness, the couple left no space in their home unattended. Their decorating effort extends beyond the main living spaces. Interior hallway walls and woodwork feature any variety of fanciful paint treatments. Kitchen countertops are artistically arranged with still lifes. Even a bedroom desk has been cleverly embellished by Anne with a trompe l'oeil ink blotter.

The hallway feeding off the entry bears the warm, glowing charm of a stained-glass window as well as a collection of strikingly displayed objets d'art and other artworks, including a self-portrait

that Anne painted when she was in college.

In the hallway leading to the dining room, the walls are art in their own right. Anne decorated them with freehand murals of her favorite Cape Cod cove and an imaginary lighthouse that's a composite of many of her favorites in Maine. "I love the sea," says Anne, whose family moved to Maine when she was 12 years old. "Living near the ocean has always been an integral part of my life."

Nautical motifs are woven throughout the home, in the form of seashell and sea-related collectibles, ship models, seascape paintings, and Anne's own decorative paintwork on furnishings, as well as walls. When it

🔥

*Opposite: Personal style at the table translates as an ensemble of rare antique Czech rose bowls, an old pansy glove box, Maine pottery, and English cups and saucers.*
*Left: Vivid collections add zest to the black and white kitchen.*
*Top left: Collections include beeswax and carved animals.*
*Top right: Anne's mother hooked the floral rug.*

# CINDERELLA STORY

came time, in 1987, for Anne to use her artistry in a commercial capacity, the resulting shop was named Turnip & Brigs. Kate, the couple's daughter, "was in love with the word 'turnip,' which represents land," explains Anne. "And I chose the word 'brigs,' which represents the sea.

Land and sea meant that I could sell anything."

Although Anne enjoys her shop, it's at her home that she paints and showcases some of her most inventive creations.

The room that serves as her pièce de résistance is the upstairs bedroom—a study in white, decorated

with collectibles and yard-sale finds Anne made one-of-a-kind with her decorative paintwork.

Originally occupied by the carriage house caretaker, the room was replete with a working fireplace and its original marble mantel when the Klapfishes bought the

building. "I love to light a fire on a winter Sunday afternoon and go upstairs to read," says Anne.

But for the rest of the year, she wants the room to feel like a summer bedroom by the sea—thus, the breezy white paint everywhere and casual smattering of hooked rugs.

Much of Anne's fine art decorates the mantel, and her more informal creativity is evident nearly everywhere else: on the papier-mâché angels crowning a window; the ship on the back of a desk; and even the bed tray.

With a sharp eye and the wave of her paintbrush, Anne has swept the carriage house with all the enchantment of a fairy tale. □

*Top right and opposite: A yard-sale desk becomes functional art with Anne's trompe l'oeil blotter and decorative paint trim.*
*Left: Indian sweetgrass baskets and Staffordshire pottery ornament an old cupboard.*
*Top left: Maurice made this chest for nautical memorabilia.*

# Building the Country House

Photographs: Bradley Olman.

Left: *Terri Mallory relaxes between projects.*

Far left: *To expand the living space, the master bedroom opens onto this rear porch.*

Below: *Terri helped build the fence and rails.*

# View from a Veranda

*The broad porches at Terri Mallory's home embrace callers with cool shade and bid them welcome in a gracious Southern manner.*

On early spring afternoons in Stone Mountain, Georgia, during the interlude between the sometimes nasty chill of winter and the scorching summer heat, Terri Mallory often makes a solitary escape to her tranquil new veranda.

Her thoughts may carry her back five years to the day when magazine pictures of a Louisiana low-country house built about 1900 caught her

**BY STEVE COOPER**
**PRODUCED BY RUTH REITER**

71

**Right:** *Interior transoms and a painted canvas runner set boundaries for the main entry between the dining room and the music room.*

**Far right:** *By slightly angling furnishings, the family room's seating area is more appealing than furniture simply lined up in an ordinary fashion parallel to the walls.*

**Below:** *Using assorted stock molding, Terri improvised the mantel around the granite fireplace.*

attention. It was a variation of the French Colonial style, introduced by settlers along the Mississippi River in the 18th century and often referred to as plantation style. The hipped roof, with its steeply pitched, broad slopes, was its most distinctive feature. The roof was propped by fetching, chamfered posts, and it shaded generous windows, French doors, and the spacious veranda.

"I saw the pictures and knew I wanted to build that house," Terri says.

As planned, the new Georgia exterior looks almost identical to the Louisiana original. But inside, Terri created her own floor plan with open rooms, high ceilings, and architectural details, such as columns matching the porch posts.

"I wanted my home to be like my grandmother's: a place where I could sit outside and rock on the front porch," the native Southerner says.

For several years, Terri had been thinking of building such a home. Early in her life, an interest in construction was sparked by her father, Lewis Mallory, now a semiretired mechanical engineer. He introduced her to painting, carpentry, and other grimy realities of the building process.

**Right:** *Wide mullions in kitchen cabinet doors are a detail repeated in the home's many windows.*

**Far right:** *Opening onto the family room, the kitchen is somewhat enclosed by a cooktop island serving as a partition. Traffic flows freely around it.*

**Below:** *The eating area adjacent to the kitchen has antique heart-of-pine floors below and a tongue-and-groove plank ceiling above.*

By the early 1980s—when she was just into her 20s—she was tackling projects of her own. She began renovating old houses while living in Charlotte, North Carolina, and eventually completed four restorations.

"Building a house from the ground up seemed the next logical step," she says.

After she chanced upon the picture of the plantation house she wanted, she enlisted her father's help. They worked side by side along with contractor Charles Slappey of Hoschton, Georgia, to build her new house.

"I was here every day digging ditches and helping lay pipe, and Dad and I built all the fencing and the interior trim plinth blocks," she says.

Though this saved money, Terri didn't pick up a shovel for the sake of a few dollars. She sought a more tangible reward.

She says, "I find it fun to create something. My real profession is investing, so I work with intangibles all the time. But with building, the reward is right in front of you. We would start framing a wall in the morning and by afternoon we saw our creation take shape."

In a more favorable economy, she could envision herself launching a full-time building career.

# View from a Veranda

UPPER LEVEL

MAIN LEVEL

**Right:** *The steel frame and wooden treads of the double stairway should stand up to harsh winter weather.*

**Left:** *Terri's floor plan can easily allow for five bedrooms.*

**Below:** *The master bedroom is on the home's main level, providing easy access to the veranda.*

"I enjoy being involved physically. This project was a wonderful way to create and see rewards immediately," she says.

Certainly, there's much to admire in Terri's house—from the amiable architecture to the rooms-with-a-view floor plan she penned herself.

Downstairs, Terri has divided space into three zones. In the front she placed two formal rooms for entertaining and dining. To the rear is a family room/kitchen/

eating area just off an outside porch. As a retreat, there's a main-floor master bedroom suite.

"I always wanted my bedroom on the first level. It's more convenient, and I can step out onto the porch when it's nice," Terri says.

Depending on how the upstairs space is used, there is room for as many as four bedrooms.

Enhancing the simple, easy-living layout is a decorating style that is elegant and refined, yet is also ingratiating and seems to invite guests to sit a spell. Assisting Terri in balancing formal and casual elements was designer Jacque Campbell of Roswell, Georgia.

Thoughtful details include the handsome shaping of interior columns; the aged, warm color of recycled heart-pine floors; planked ceilings rising to more than 10 feet; and the manner in which rooms flow together in pristine whites, hot pinks, and luxurious blues.

Terri's favorite spot is the broad back porch. She's particularly proud of the complex two-story, double stairway she built. The rear exterior perfectly evokes the mood of the Louisiana low-country plantation house she sought to create.

She says, "If you want me, you'll find me out back on the porch." □

Floor plan illustration: Carson Ode

# June

# SEASONS ON THE SOUND

*Each summer the Millers head east to their Victorian home on an island off Long Island, where the days take on a lazy rhythm all their own.*

Only 2½ hours from their home in Westchester, New York, George and Shane Miller pursue a summer lifestyle on an island that belies the proximity of the two locations. Days at their sunbathed Victorian summer house suggest a much greater remoteness than the sprint down (or, in traffic, crawl along) the Long Island Freeway might indicate.

And in truth, there *is* a little more isolation involved: The short trip between full-time and summer houses entails not only road but water. The Millers' second home is located on an island of charming turn-of-the-century and earlier houses, with a shoreline washed by Long Island waters. Access, after the freeway, is only by ferry or boat.

Although the Millers' house isn't waterfront property, its location on a bluff just across the street affords a dazzling view of the sound, especially of sailboats bobbing at their docks and of sunlight playing shadow games with the water. Everything about the Miller place, in fact, seems to bespeak sun and summer: Even the house's clapboards are a rosy paint shade reminiscent of the season's first sunburn.

The airy appeal already was in place when the Millers purchased the circa-1890 house. Not only was no restoration work required, but virtually no cosmetic changes were needed either. "When we walked into the house five years ago, all we needed to move in was a toothbrush," says Shane.

**BY CANDACE ORD MANROE**

*Left: These days, while her husband, George, is away on business, Shane Miller adapts to the empty nest: Between them, the couple has 12 children.*

*Below: The Millers' house, which dates to 1890, exudes period charm with its gingerbread trim, fanciful colonnaded and pedimented porch, and center gables.*

Photographs: Tony Giammarino. Produced with Mona Dworkin.

*The front porch of the Miller home is a prelude to what follows indoors—flowers everywhere. White wicker and soft floral fabrics also reflect the casual country style found inside.*

# SUMMER LIVING

For eight years, the family had rented a summerhouse in Southampton. During that time, they visited—and fell in love with—the island they now call home throughout the summer months as well as on weekends and holidays.

"Once we would come across on the ferry, we could feel our shoulders drop with relaxation," recalls Shane.

Their intrigue with the island prompted the Millers to rent a barn there for a season. While renting, they found and bought the blushing Victorian. "We just knew we liked it here that much," explains Shane. "We wouldn't be going anywhere else."

Part of the appeal of the island is its relative lack of development. A few narrow roads cavort and twist across it as though they were getting away with something. At every turn are scenic vistas, be they historic homes or the best of nature.

Most of the amenities of city life are missing. There are only a handful of restaurants (and not all are open all the time), no movie theaters, and not one shopping mall. The islanders resoundingly applaud this, believing their time is better spent on the hiking path, biking up a particularly taxing hill, or picking up a few things for dinner from the island's health-food store.

Shane and George had no trouble acclimating to the island rhythms. Having backgrounds as physical therapists, they both knew the value of activities that keep the body healthy and supple. "I spend a lot of my time

Above: *Even the elegantly carved living room mantel and fireplace are given a breath of sweet summer air with bouquets of flowers in a basket and vase, a decorating theme that's repeated throughout the Millers' home.*

*Lace panels on the windows, topped with shirred floral valances, create a gentle romanticism in the living room, while still admitting ample natural light.*

# SUMMER LIVING

Left: *Already
decorated in
Shane's favorite
colors, the kitchen
sold the Millers on
the house. Country
style takes a
contemporary turn
here with clean-
lined furnishings;
warmth emanates
from the tablecloth
and flowers.*

Below: *A tin of
flowers, a silk
shawl, and
puddling sheer
curtains make a
striking still life in
the dining room.*

here in the summer walking, biking, or going to the beach," says Shane. George's business obligations (Shane helps George run a physical therapy equipment business) give him less time to master Shane's range of pastimes. But he still manages to fit in plenty of time to fish.

As a couple, the Millers tend the grounds of their island home with purpose and passion. "One of George's and my greatest loves is flowers," says Shane. "We may even be a little manic about it." Not only do they garden outdoors at the summer place, they bring more than a bit of the garden onto the porch and indoors.

"I like to feel that there's a garden on the porch," Shane says. As part of this, the couple has their own traveling hibiscus tree. "We take it home in the fall and bring it back in the summer," Shane says. "At the garden shop, we buy so much we can't fit it all in our car."

The Millers' love of flowers manifests itself as

a major decorating theme in their home. Creamware country pitchers ariot with cuttings from the garden accessorize tables and desks. More formal vases bring the blooming fragrance and color of summer to the mantels. Woven baskets and metal buckets filled with ever-changing bouquets are plopped right on the floor, as doorstops or organic soft sculptures of sorts.

Like a contagion, the flower motif spread throughout the home once the Millers moved in. Fabric selection was easy: floral prints. Art selection was easy: flower and still-life paintings by the couple's close friend, Olive Reich, a talented watercolorist whose summer home is just across the street. (When not negotiating artwork, the two women enjoy visiting on Olive's deck overlooking the water.)

Work done on the home by previous owners blended beautifully with the Millers' personal style. The soft pink of the exterior paint was a

*Thanks to the island breeze, dining room French doors can be flung open to capture the porch's garden effect. In addition to garden cuttings, Shane brings in sunflowers and whatever else catches her eye at the florist's.*

# SUMMER LIVING

natural for the pastel fabrics the couple had in mind for the furnishings indoors and on the porch. The home's French doors and other woodwork already were painted white, and the hardwood floors were pickled a pale, sandy hue, enhancing the feeling of sunshine and seashore the Millers wanted to impart.

Even the kitchen—often the toughest room to approve—was on target with the Millers' taste. "I love blue and white," says Shane, "so that's a theme throughout the house. This kitchen already was blue and white. As soon as I walked in, I thought it was made for me."

As long as she can remember, Shane has been fond of wicker. With its breezy, whitewashed style, the island house offered an opportunity to indulge that predilection to its fullest. White wicker furnishes every room as chairs, desks, tables, and vanities.

"We did get an overstuffed chair in the living room for George," says Shane. But even this departure was due to practicality, not preference, to provide adequate leg room for George's tall frame.

Besides being a retreat for relaxing, the house serves as a gathering place for family—and, between their visits, a place to adjust to the empty nest. Combined, the couple has 12 children, the youngest of whom just entered college. "The house is wonderful because all the kids can visit at the same time," Shane says. "I miss the routine of children at home and am restructuring my life with an empty nest. Being here helps." □

Above: *One daughter's bedroom is filled with whimsy, from the old painted iron bed topped with a colorful quilt to the wicker writing table outfitted with a tea tray and crowned with one of Shane's hats and some dried flowers. Simple bows tied in the center give the curtains a distinctive, soft yet simple look.*

*Dressed in sunshine colors, a guest bedroom has the appeal of early morning. Gauzy half-panels are all that's needed for the upstairs windows. Art is by neighbor Olive Reich.*

SUMMER LIVING

*The Allreds describe their mountain property as paradise and there seems no reason to disagree.*
*Ron says, "The beauty of this region is unmatched. There's no place we'd rather be."*

# SUMMER LIVING

# WHEN COMPANY CALLS

*Friends staying at the idyllic Rocky Mountain retreat of Ron and Joyce Allred often spot deer grazing near the log cabin. It's the nature of the place.*

Right: *If there's a natural habitat for Ron and Joyce Allred, this is it: the woods outside their cabin.*

Below: *Nestled into the San Juan Mountain forest, the Allreds' cabin seems a secluded retreat. But it's only a stone's throw from a ski run.*

If you've ever dreamed of pristine mountain streams, pine trees gently dancing to the rhythm of a cool breeze, and craggy cliffs majestically towering above mountain valleys, your vision probably captured the feel of Telluride, Colorado.

At 8,750 feet high in the Rocky Mountains, this gem of a town was spurred into existence by a gold mining bonanza during the 1880s. It's undergoing another boom today as a destination for skiers, tourists, and celebrities.

Among those staking their claim to this breathtaking terrain are Ron and Joyce Allred, drawn here 14 years ago.

"There aren't many places left in the world that you can call paradise," Joyce says, "but this is one of them."

During their first 10 years here, the couple lived in town with their seven children. But four years ago—with their children grown—they began developing a 7-acre property located about 5 miles outside of Telluride.

Their land is part of Mountain Village Ski Resort, where Ron is director of development.

When the Allreds began building, they constructed a cozy log cabin and lived there for two years before moving into a more spacious house a few hundred feet up their hill.

But the cabin, now a guesthouse, is still treasured by the Allreds.

"It's a perfect spot for me," says Ron. "It's a five-minute walk from the cabin down to my

By Steve Cooper
Produced by Sue Mattes

Photographs: Laurie E. Dickson.

87

Left: *Most of the log cabin is open to view from the hearth, including the sleeping loft above the kitchen and dining area. Joyce says, "I've used a few antiques as accessories. But I didn't want to use too many because I didn't want a guesthouse that functions like an antique." Windows and doors were all built at the site.*

office, or, in the winter, I can ski to work."

Log construction allows for large, unobstructed spaces such as the guest cabin's living room, dining area, and kitchen, which actually form a single open area. This impression of volume is reinforced by the high ceiling and towering stone fireplace.

Furnishings were kept as simple as the structure itself. Guests may find themselves dreaming away afternoons while curled up on an overstuffed, floral-patterned love seat in front of the fireplace. Or they may prefer the gracefully shaped twig chairs.

Though compact, the kitchen is fully equipped. A small range and a counter-height refrigerator are the main concessions to tight quarters.

Overlooking the living room is a sleeping loft with a pair of beds. A shedlike, stone-clad addition was

erected at the rear of the cabin to house a master bedroom suite. The rock for these walls was blasted from an old quarry only minutes from the cabin.

Joyce says, "It's the perfect little mountain cabin. We can sleep six comfortably, and we've always got someone here."

A log structure was an appropriate choice for this setting adjacent to ski runs. Though rugged and rustic, the facade has an Old West charm.

It's a direct descendant of the frontier cabins that were once home to trappers, miners, and ranchers. Constructed by stacking logs on logs and rocks on rocks, it evokes a frugal elegance. It's the same sensible beauty reflected in the red flannel, blue denim, and leather boots of the West.

How fitting, then, that the architecture was inspired by a guest cabin

*The cabin is as warm as it looks, says Joyce's son, Tom Fulton, who has stayed there with his wife, Wendy. He adds, "It's a very tight house. Very snug. Put a couple of logs on the fire, and you're set for the night."*

SUMMER LIVING

belonging to fashion mogul Ralph Lauren. Joyce was smitten by the all-American style of Lauren's renovated, historical cabin when she visited his 12,000-acre ranch in the southern Colorado community of Ridgeway.

"It was exactly what I'd been looking for. A small, cozy, warm cabin that looked like it belonged up here in the Rocky Mountains. I definitely didn't want anything that looked like it belonged in the city, and Ralph Lauren's guest cabin was adorable," Joyce says.

The Allreds' version is a modest 1,100 square feet. It was constructed by builder Corey Fortenberry using hand-peeled, hand-notched lodgepole pine timbers up to 35 feet in length, from Alpine Log Homes of Victor, Montana.

"All the logs were taken from standing dead timbers, so no living trees had to be cut," Corey says.

Ever since Ron and Joyce moved up the hill, the cabin has been used mostly by their children. Joyce's son, Tom Fulton, and his wife, Wendy, lived there while constructing their own home.

"It was wonderful being tucked away in the woods," Tom says. "Sometimes a five-foot wall of snow would build up around the house and you'd feel like you were living back in the old mountain days—but with all the conveniences."

Because logs are heavy and dense, the interior is invitingly quiet. To hear the sound of the breeze rustling through the pines, a window must be opened.

Often, there are visits from local wildlife. Deer greet guests, blue jays come calling, and squirrels chatter at the door.

"It's peaceful, but never dull," Joyce says.

And if there's a chill in the air, there's always wood for the fireplace.

Joyce says, "With the logs and the scent of the forest and a fire going, it's a very romantic place." □

Above: *The loft can easily sleep four.*

Below: *When Joyce's now-75-year-old aunt, Helen Young, of Florence, Colorado, was a girl, she pieced together the top of the quilt seen in this master bedroom. It was stored for 50 years.*

*Cabin kitchens often are neglected because of tight space and budgets. But the Allreds planned for full-time living by including such amenities as a dishwasher. Ron says, "I wouldn't have minded living here forever."*

# SUMMER LIVING

*A home entertainer to the core, Pat uses the deck as a stage for cold buffets for friends. She dressed up the iron chairs' plywood seats with foam and fabric—"gift-wrap" style.*

# SUMMER LIVING

# ROMANCING THE RENTAL

*Decorating author Pat Ross used ingenuity to transform the Connecticut house her family rented for the summer into a place that smacks of home.*

Right: *After 20 years of owning a second home, Pat Ross decided it was time to rent.*

Below: *Her ideal rental property was a former tavern that's a registered historical landmark in Norfolk, Connecticut. Pat gave the home a few personal touches to make it the perfect getaway.*

Whenever Pat Ross stays overnight in a hotel, she transforms her surroundings in some way to reflect her personal style. The change can be no more than a tweak—a colorful scarf draped over a lampshade or a bucketful of fresh flowers plopped on the dresser. Or, it can be quite large—like the time Pat used masking tape to hang a newly purchased quilt on the wall of an especially dingy and depressing motel room.

It's no wonder, then, that Pat made some substantive, though quick and easy, decorative changes in the home she rented for the summer for herself and her family, whenever they had free time to join her.

"I knew that small personal touches could make a big difference," says Pat. "I realized that [they] could soon make this already charming house seem like home."

The rental's charm began with its location— the woodland countryside of Norfolk, Connecticut,

which Pat discovered while scouting homes for her most recent book, *Formal Country Entertaining.*

"After owning a summer home on the ocean for twenty years, I welcomed the chance to trade beach grass and scrub pines for sheltering shade trees and rolling hills as a summer renter," says Pat. When a historic colonial home on the Norfolk village green became available for rental, she didn't think twice. "The spacious home with its many guest rooms and its eclectic mix

**BY CANDACE ORD MANROE**
**PRODUCED BY PEGGY FISHER**

Photographs: Langdon Clay.

93

of English and American antiques seemed just my cup of tea," says Pat, whose earlier best-selling book, *Formal Country* (published in 1989), established her as a decorating maven, especially in country design circles.

Pat was especially impressed with the sunny living room. Its tall windows faced the village green, and, at the back, overlooked a large deck that emptied onto a field and pond. "That's where I decided to set up my office. I liked hearing the Yale students on their way to class at the Yale Music School across the road and the village church bells tolling every quarter hour," says Pat.

So much going for it, yet the house needed more before Pat could feel truly comfortable. "I was unprepared for the life of a renter. Suddenly I felt like a stranger at a charming inn," she explains.

Keeping in mind the terms of the lease and her short-term budget, Pat launched her campaign to personalize the Connecticut summer house before she even left her apartment in New York.

She refreshed her memory of the rental through snapshots. Then, to complement the summer place, she packed a few accessories of her own—a small woven rug, extra fabric for pillow slipcovers, a favorite vase, some family photographs, and a couple of quilts, one of which she would use to warm the rental's formal velvet Empire sofa.

Once in the home, she enticed friends over with pasta and garlic bread, then supervised a furniture rearrangement in the living room.

"That [rearranging furniture] is certainly the simplest and most effective way to begin," says Pat. "The furniture grouping around the fireplace gave way to a more open look with more room for guests to move about at parties."

Creating the best traffic flow was important, since Pat knew she would be using the rental for casual entertaining throughout

*The formal velvet Empire sofa is given a casual touch with Pat's blue and white quilt. Pat rolled up and stored the rental house's Oriental rugs in closets. She replaced one here with a woven rug.*

# SUMMER LIVING

Left: *Photos from home personalize the desk, along with a new watercolor-painted lampshade made by Pat's friend, Charles Muise.*

Below: *On the windows, Pat used wired French ribbon as tiebacks to allow more sunlight and yards of romantic cotton lace (which she took back to New York).*

the summer, even if only for cold buffets among small groups of friends.

An airy, summer ambience was another of Pat's priorities. She was able to lighten the house considerably, removing much of its somber mien simply by rolling up the scores of Oriental rugs that dotted the floors and storing them in closets.

Dried flower arrangements—a safe, year-round accessory— were next to go. With a perennial garden bursting with blooms, there was no need to relegate the house to a non-seasonal status, Pat reasoned.

She used a soft touch in changing existing pieces: "I knew I couldn't change anything that couldn't be changed back." On a wing

chair's pillows, for example, she basted a light, summery plaid cotton fabric over a more serious, wintry needlepoint design, and pinked ruffles around the pillow fabric's edges to preclude the need for machine sewing. A faded lampshade on a desk didn't provide much inspiration, so Pat remedied that, too. Using the old shade for a pattern, a weekend guest made a new shade from heavy paper, then painted it.

With her stamp on the rental, Pat was free to enjoy the quietude of the New England village and even write some fiction. Best of all, when summer ended, her exit was as breezy as the vacation itself, with only pleasant memories as baggage. □

*Pat's handsome 19th-century quilt adds color to the bedroom. The pillows also are hers—a personal item that's a necessity, she says, no matter where you are.*

# SUMMER LIVING

# Up a Creek

*On the bank of Canasawacta Creek in central New York,* **Country Home**® *editors help transform a 1920s barn into a vacation house.*

Left: *Waters flow past the picnic patio of a home radically remodeled by builder Dave Kepner.*

Below right: *On sunny days, the deck and patio serve as an outside living area. Architectural lines of the house are barnlike in their simplicity.*

Bottom right: *Dave lifted this nondescript school bus barn off its crumbling foundation with a crane, set it on a new foundation, and expanded it to full two-story height.*

Table and chairs:
  Amish Country Collection
Patio brick and tile:
  Summitville Tiles, Inc.
Siding: Alcoa Building Products
Deck furniture: Cedar Shop
Doors and windows:
  Andersen Windows, Inc.
Paint throughout:
  Sherwin-Williams Co.

*D*ark clouds are breaking up overhead and the downpour is over. Where gloom prevailed moments earlier, hopeful glints of sunlight flash off the swollen stream behind the weekend retreat created by builder Dave Kepner and *Country Home* magazine.

The scene is so tranquil and the sounds so soothing, you can almost feel your heart rate slowing and your blood pressure dropping.

Dave says, "If this lot had been a block from the creek, it never would have interested me."

Even with the stream, the property still required a buyer with Dave's flair for spotting the jewel amidst the junk. The lot's beauty was blemished by a homely, 1920s barn erected to shelter two school buses.

**By Steve Cooper**
**Interior Design by Michael Graham**
**Produced by Ann Maine and Peggy Fisher**

Left: *Dave gave the living room a sense of size beyond its actual proportions by flooding the room with light and opening the ceiling a full two stories. By decorating with such items as bait signs,* Country Home *designers caught the spirit of the vacation home.*

Above: *Dave and Cristina Kepner moved in when the project was completed.*

Upholstered furniture:
  La-Z-Boy Chair Co.
Fireplace: Vermont
  Castings, Inc.
Signs: Garden Source
  Furnishings, Inc.
Creels: Palecek
Additional pillows: Manderley
Rug: Woodard Weave at
  Thos K. Woodard
Blanket: L.L.Bean, Inc.
Antique fishing tackle:
  Lady Paydacker Antiques

"It sure wasn't much to look at, but I saw a possibility," says Dave. "You might say I sort of have a thing for old barns."

One of Dave's earlier projects—the resurrection of a 200-year-old barn in Remsenburg, New York—was published in *Country Home* in August 1989.

The current project is also in New York. But it stands beside Canasawacta Creek in Norwich, a small, rural town.

Most traces of the barn's former, oil-stained incarnation are gone. The house now blooms as an ideal escape for harried urbanites, such as Dave and his wife, Cristina, who live on Long Island. Dave will stay at the house when in Norwich to work on a housing project he is developing here.

"I couldn't be more pleased with the way this has turned out. Unless people already knew what it had been, I don't think anyone could imagine a couple of school buses used

*Up a Creek*

Left: *Mealtimes are accompanied by the lovely melody of the passing stream. Dining is only a few steps from the kitchen.*

Above: *What the kitchen lacks in size, it makes up for with the latest in refrigerator, range, and dishwasher designs, and handsome cabinetry. As a reminder of the home's past as a school bus barn, the sink is a bold, primary red.*

Appliances: Frigidaire Co.
Cabinets throughout: Merillat Industries, Inc.
Plumbing fixtures throughout: Eljer Industries
Fish plates, mugs: Vietri, Inc.
Table, chairs: Judson Creek Antiques
Pine cupboard: The Mad Hatter Antiques

to be parked in this house," Dave says.

Of course, before the project, few could imagine the bus garage as a house.

As is often true when building, obtaining construction permits was difficult. Because the structure sat only 30 feet back from the stream, local officials were concerned about flooding during heavy storms. For this reason, current building codes demand new homes be kept more than 100 feet away from a creek. But Dave argued that the less stringent, 1920s rules should apply because he was renovating an existing structure.

"The possibility of having this house right up against the stream was why I bought the property in the first place. It would have had no appeal for me if the house had to move back," Dave says.

He wrangled with local government for 12 months, hiring surveyors, hydrologists, and other experts who could assess the possibility of a deluge sweeping across the lot. In the end, he received permission for the structure to remain within 30 feet of the creek if a new, modified foundation was built.

That problem solved, Dave faced another issue: Only a story-and-a-half tall, the barn couldn't accommodate an upper story, which Dave believed the cottage would need.

So a few feet from the bus barn, Dave built a new foundation identical in size to the original. Around its perimeter, he erected a wood-framed, 7-foot wall open to the sky.

Then, on an autumn day, with an audience of amazed 6-year-olds from the neighborhood

*Up a Creek*

Left: *At the foot of the elaborately detailed rustic bed in the master bedroom are a pair of built-in drawers. Giving walls a pine-plank treatment adds to an already woodsy mood.*

Above: *An Amish quilt design was adapted for the tile pattern of the master bathroom. The diamond-shaped window was placed above the whirlpool tub to allow additional light into the room.*

Bed: Ken Heitz
Curtain fabric: Waverly Fabrics
Lamp: Shoal Creek

*Up a Creek*

grammar school watching, workers freed the barn from its foundation, brought in a towering crane, and hoisted the structure onto a new, half-wall foundation.

Completing the makeover took a few more months. The house was wrapped in a new type of siding that promises years of maintenance-free service without fading.

Inside, architect Richard Jankowski of Oxford, New York, has created a barn-simple layout. The living room, dining room, and kitchen are perfectly perched to provide a view through two sets of sliding, glass doors.

With the renovation complete, Dave turned to the design team from *Country Home* magazine for help with interiors to create the kind of sophisticated, small-scale retreat gaining in popularity.

Adding design touches echoing the home's history was the first step. Primary colors splashed here and there in fixtures, paint, and tiles are a reminder of its school ties.

Because it's a vacation house, rooms were kept carefree and serene. A few well-placed bait signs, tackle boxes, and fishing rods signal that this is a stress-free zone.

The home's breezy attitude is enhanced by an airy and open living room with a ceiling reaching the full two stories. Adding to the casual atmosphere is a cast-iron, porcelain-enamel fireplace mounted on a raised hearth. Because a chimney would have been intrusive, an easily vented, natural gas-fueled fireplace was chosen. Upholstered wing chairs give the room a hint of formality.

Left: *Applying such a
strong wall color
helps set this home
office apart from the
rest of the house.
When business is
done, the room offers
a quiet reading spot
or a place to house
overnight guests. The
love seat folds out
into a bed.*

Below right: *The new
garage shown in this
floor plan was erected
about where the bus
barn once stood.*

Bench and table:
 Maine Cottage Furniture, Inc.
Fax machine:
 Sharp Electronics Corp.

Though small, the kitchen is fully
equipped. The newly designed appliances
have slight curves softening their edges,
and their energy efficiency has been
increased.

Also downstairs are a small bedroom and
a home office/guest bedroom. The office
cabinetry is custom quality, though assem-
bled from stock components.

The entire second floor is a master bedroom suite. It features a colorful bathroom
with a tile pattern inspired by an Amish
quilt. There's also a whirlpool tub.

It's been a remarkable transformation for
Dave's former school bus barn. It's gone
from fail to pass, from F to A, and from
winter midterms to summer vacation. □

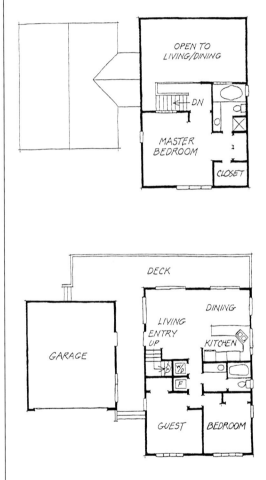

## Up a Creek

Floor plan illustration: Carson Ode

# Rose
## REINCARNATE

*Old garden roses—in all their sumptuous glory—are born again at Mike Shoup's Antique Rose Emporium.*

Revelations seldom occur along the Texas roadside, where the occasional car whizzes by and the air quivers with heat above the blacktop. But such was the setting for a vision that would irrevocably alter Mike Shoup's life.

A trained horticulturalist, Mike had always shunned roses as too finicky and delicate for the tough Texas climate—until he saw a pale yellow cloud of them engulfing a fence along the edge of a rural road, far from the tender care of any gardener.

"It was late summer," recalls Mike, "and not even the sweltering Texas heat could stop that rose."

Local rosarians examined cuttings of the feisty plant and deemed it a Mermaid, an English variety from 1918.

Of such discoveries converts are made.

Venturing out from his hometown of Independence on a grand web of byways between Austin and Houston, Mike soon turned up other varieties growing contentedly—along the roadsides, on abandoned properties, and in old

**By Charlotte Forbes. Produced by Linda Joan Smith**

Left: *This romantic bouquet includes the peppermint-striped Variegata di Bologna (a Bourbon rose dating to 1909) and the lush pink Madame Berkeley (a tea rose from 1899).*

Above: *Mike Shoup and his wife, Jean, at the Antique Rose Emporium.*

Right: *Mike frequently finds old roses surviving in rural graveyards.*

Photographs: William N. Hopkins, Hopkins Associates

Left: *The white rose that adds luster to the Emporium's cottage garden is the polyantha Marie Pavié and dates to 1888. Clothing the picket fence in pink is the Zéphirine Drouhin, a Bourbon rose from the Civil War era.*

Below: *The climbing rose Fun Juan Lo thrives on this arbor.*

cemeteries. Without fail, these hardy survivors were yesterday's roses, supplanted more than 100 years ago by florist-perfect hybrids and all but unknown to today's gardeners. What's more, these heirloom blossoms of claret-tinged eggshell, dusky pink, butter yellow, and vermilion—fragrant blooms that once charmed royalty and inspired poets—were flourishing without a lick of pruning or spraying, their only caretaker Mother Nature.

Just as the horticulturist in Mike applauded the garden virtues of these and other old-fashioned roses, the romantic in him was seduced by their beauty and connection to the past. Among them, after all, were Empress Josephine's luxuriant blooms from

Malmaison; the voluptuous cabbage roses of Victorian still lifes; the sweetbrier of Shakespeare's *A Midsummer Night's Dream*; and the red and white damask, symbol of the War of the Roses.

Identifying the anonymous beauties in his own growing collection often was slow going for Mike. Those roses found along the roadside had no provenance, and even the specimens growing in private gardens had long ago lost their names. Until the mysteries of their breeding could be solved, Mike gave each of the blooms under study "found" names, usually linked to the road, town, or gardener from where or whom the cuttings of the roses came.

Often, happy surprises

*The white rose that adds luster to the Emporium's cottage garden is the polyantha Marie Pavié and dates to 1888. Clothing the picket fence in pink is the Zéphirine Drouhin, a Bourbon rose from the Civil War era.*

ensued: the cabbagelike white rose, temporarily dubbed the Eloise Adams after its Louisiana donor, was later proclaimed the Coltilde Soupert, a polyantha rose of French fame that dates to the 1890s.

In 1983 Mike went public with his passion by founding the Antique Rose Emporium, and in 1985 the Emporium's now-vast display gardens took root. Those gardens today are bright with roses that cascade from trellises, climb up pillars, cluster in cottage gardens, and paint brilliant waves of color against the big Texas sky. There are more than 200 varieties for sale on the property as well as by mail.

Mike is quick to note that not all the roses are "old roses," officially defined as those flourishing before 1867, when La France, the first hybrid tea rose, was introduced. Although some Emporium flowers do go back centuries, others have histo-

ries of less than 50 years.

"When we do find newer varieties with old garden rose qualities—generous blossoms and foliage, good fragrance, hardiness, and the ability to be a workhorse in the garden—we sell them," says Mike.

It's the old garden roses, however, that come with a taproot into local history. Ask Mike about the pioneering days of the Lone Star State and he'll probably refer you to his Republic of Texas Collection. Featuring roses that flourished locally between 1836 and 1845—the prestatehood years when Texas was a republic—the collection stars Louis Philippe, a regal crimson and white rose imported from Paris by the republic's first statesman to France.

Many other old roses also survived the long ocean voyage to the New World, brought by settlers hoping to replicate the gardens they had left behind. As home-

steaders slowly moved west across the continent, they uprooted their precious roses time and again, wrapping burlap around their roots, or they took cuttings of their favorites and stuck them in potatoes to keep them alive.

"In Texas towns that sprang up along wagon train routes, you often see a rose called Harison's Yellow," says Mike. Known by many as the Yellow Rose of Texas, it's also in the Republic Collection.

Though old roses now are readily available through the Emporium and a number of other nurseries, the most romantic—and perhaps most fitting—way to come by many varieties remains the "rose rustling" by which Mike got his start. "The great thing about rose rustling is that you only find roses that are thriving in your area," says Mike. Many garden groups now sponsor these treasure hunts for old-time roses, which are great fun and a good way for beginners to learn to identify old rose types.

After years of fighting alongside other old-rose lovers to resurrect these robust and charming plants, Mike now sees an upsurge of interest across the country. Currently, the Emporium's roses flourish in gardens from the Caribbean to Alaska, and the hardworking staff can barely keep up with the demand. Even rose breeders are taking note of the shift in tastes and are veering away from fussy hybrid teas to breed new varieties that mimic the inborn strengths of the old rose: resistance to disease, a great diversity of forms, versatility in the garden, and an intoxicating scent that whispers of the ages. □

# August

# Family Time

By Steve Cooper
Produced by
Mary Anne Thomson

*Spirits are revived and the stresses of city life are left behind when the Willmans break away to their century-old cottage near the Mississippi River. It was much the same for the Methodist families who built this riverside Chautauqua community long ago.*

Photographs: William N. Hopkins, Hopkins Associates

Right: *Sonja created
an eclectic treat in
the living room
by mixing prints
and vivid colors.*

Left: *Bob and Sonja
Willman picnic
with their children,
Justin and Ashley.
The family's woody
is a 1949 DeSoto.
Stones for the porch
columns (inset) came
from nearby creek
beds.*

Below: *A pair of
Staffordshire dogs
stand guard over
Sonja's living
room display.*

In an idyllic world, Mom sips the lemonade her husband brought to her so she wouldn't have to interrupt a good, long read. Dad putters with his favorite toy, a pristine automobile built 40 years ago. The kids? They're down at the riverbank watching the pollywogs grow hind legs.

This would be a daydream for most people. But for Bob and Sonja Willman and their children, it's just another summer weekend spent at their vacation cottage near Alton, Illinois.

"I feel my blood pressure drop ten points every time I drive up," Bob says.

The cottage is located within a community of 150 small homes nestled near the shore of the Mississippi River. The Willmans' house sits beside a creek about a block from the big river.

The site was developed as a Methodist Chautauqua camp in the early 1890s. Here faithful families invested

*Family Time*

their summer months in the pursuit of spiritual, intellectual, and physical development. Children might enjoy a day of Bible study, crafts, and swimming while the adults were exhorted by a preacher or enlightened by entertainers performing classical drama or satire.

Bob says, "Prior to the days of working mothers, women and children would come and spend the entire summer here while the husbands commuted back and forth from Springfield, Illinois, or St. Louis, Missouri."

Initially, only a few cabins were built. For shelter, tents were pitched on wooden platforms erected to keep families high and dry. As years passed, these camp sites became

115

homesites, and modest houses were raised.

Though it has had its ups and downs through the decades, the community has settled into a mellow maturity as a nonsectarian retreat. In a time when life seems to pull this way and that, here is a refuge seemingly devoid of menace, meanness, or ill manners.

"It's like a camp for families," Sonja says. "There's a

very relaxed, friendly atmosphere where there's always something to do for everyone, and people are always watching out for the safety of our two children. In fact, if the kids were to hurt themselves, one of the neighbors would probably pick them up, clean any cuts, and send them home all bandaged up. It's that kind of place."

Sonja escapes here for most of the summer with the children, Justin and Ashley. The campy cottage invigorates Sonja as she designs lamps, wall coverings, and other home furnishings she plans to market. During the week, however, she must make a 45-minute commute to oversee her St. Louis gift shop, Summer House. When Bob isn't taking off for his job as an airline pilot, he also breaks away to the family's haven.

The Willmans' retreat was built in 1892 as one of the community's first permanent residences. It has changed little through the years, though a screened porch supported by columns of stacked stone replaced the original porch in the 1920s.

Sonja is particulary pleased the cabin's character has been left relatively unaltered for a century.

"It's very quiet and peaceful, and the setting is so picturesque," she

Right: *Accessories reveal a lot: The Willmans are patriots who enjoy animals, fabrics in a surprising array of patterns, and traveling.*

Left: *The cottage's diminutive size can be sensed in this view through the master bedroom into the living room. Ashley's bedroom is on the other side of the living room, and Justin's is in a loft at the rear of the cottage.*

says. "If you think about your image of a summer cottage, it probably looks a lot like ours. It's ideal."

The Willmans bought the home little more than a year ago. Before that, they owned another Chautauqua cabin for three years. Unlike their former vacation house, the new cottage is equipped with central heating so the family can visit any time of the year.

*Family Time*

As with all cottages, space is at a premium. But with an abundance of wood paneling, ample windows allowing for sunny daytime rooms, and playful interior treatments, the house is much more cozy than confining.

"All the different kinds of wood used on ceilings and walls caught my eye," Bob says. "The living room ceiling stands out to me because it's done in quadrants and it has a herringbone pattern. The unusual window detailing also gives the house a flavor all its own."

Sonja added more spice to this flavor with an eclectic blend of living room furnishings. These include an ivy-print sofa, an old twig rocker, a Chinese rug from the 1930s, a lawn-ornament squirrel on the mantel, an 1880s carved oak dresser used for display, and assorted plates, pictures, oddities, and whimsies.

"I wanted a cozy, wintry look, like it had been handed down through the years and had collected bits and pieces from all different generations. Kind of an Adirondack feeling. Campy, I guess," she says.

In addition to accumulating good antique furniture, Sonja also treks through consignment shops, secondhand stores, and garage sales looking for odds and ends with appealing character.

"I'm looking more for old, 1920s memorabilia that's fun," says Sonja. "Not the true treasures. But I might purposely look for an old piece of Staffordship with a chip or a crack—something that indicates it's a real piece

❦

Left: *The family spends much of its leisure time on the porch, which beckons with a distinctive blue-sky ceiling and grass-green floor.*

Right: *Before the Willmans perked up the color scheme, the porch was painted gray, and the flooring was indoor-outdoor carpet.*

Below: *Both Bob and Sonja were first attracted to the cottage because of its flower boxes. The planters now overflow with pansies, primroses, geraniums, and petunias.*

that people really lived with. That's a quality I enjoy."

Though few major changes were necessary, the Willmans did revamp the kitchen. They stripped old wallpaper and replaced it with wood paneling similar to that in other rooms. The dining area of the kitchen was given its own distinctive, romantic look with elegant wallpaper, pine furnishings, and a fine salvaged lamp.

A treehouse-like loft space at the back of the house also was converted into a bedroom for 12-year-old Justin. He likes having the somewhat separate quarters.

*Family Time*

"My friends can come in to wake me up without waking up everyone else, and I can watch TV as late as I want. So I like it," he says.

Justin and his family also enjoy a screened porch added to the house long ago. Most family activities shift to there when the weather is nice to take advantage of the casual comfort and spaciousness.

"The porch is the main room of the house most of the time," Sonja says. "We eat and play games out there, or read. Also, it's a very good, peaceful spot where I can spend time on my creative projects."

Fortunately, one thing that didn't come with the cottage was an enormous price tag. The home cost less than most other vacation homes the Willmans have seen.

"The cottage is a very affordable place. Inexpensive, really," says Bob. "But the primary reason we bought it had nothing to do with money."

Here, Sonja and Bob can relax. Justin has his friends. Seven-year-old Ashley can go frog watching.

Sonja says, "Buying the cottage was really all about family." □

# THE *Maine* EVENT

*For years, Don Maharam imagined escaping to a
lakeside log cabin in the wilds of Maine.
Thanks to a talented family, he has realized that dream.*

BY STEVE COOPER. PRODUCED BY BONNIE MAHARAM

As Don Maharam's canoe glides across
Maine's Sebago Lake, echoes of his most
memorable boyhood summers are as real as
the ethereal blue of the sky above, the cool
touch of a hand dipped into the icy waters,
and the sweet scent of the surrounding
forest's pine.

"I remember coming up to Maine from
New York every year for summer camp. The
area has always intrigued me and stayed
with me," Don says.

For years, he daydreamed about building
his own lakeshore home in Maine. But, as

Left: *A towering
fieldstone fireplace is
the living room's
centerpiece. The mantel
was made from the
same harvest of
Montana lodgepole-pine
logs as the walls.*

Above: *Liberal use of
glass on the rear of the
Maharam house
captures a serene view
of Sebago Lake.*

Right: *Max, a Wheaton
terrier, braves the
waters with Don and
Bonnie Maharam.*

often happens, his vision was postponed by work and circumstance. Until now.

Whenever Don and his wife, Bonnie, need to retreat from their home on hectic Long Island in New York, they set out for the more peaceful surroundings of the camp house they've built in Maine.

The 6½-hour drive takes them from congestion to calm, from pollution to paradise, and from the wild life that is New York to a completely different kind of wildlife. It's a welcome respite from Don's business in contract/architectural fabrics and Bonnie's busy schedule as a *Country Home®* magazine regional editor.

Their log cabin is a grand version of Don's recollections of his youth.

Bonnie says, "We'd always dreamed of building a home with that rustic, *On Golden Pond* feeling."

Don also refers to the movies to describe his feelings about the cabin. But instead of recalling the Henry Fonda-Katharine Hepburn film, he reaches back to Michael Caine's first major movie character.

"At this stage of my life, the Maine house was part of that 'what's-it-all-about-Alfie?' syndrome. It has fulfilled a desire I've had for quite a number of years," says Don.

To translate that desire into a log-and-stone structure, Don turned to the family's building experts. Plans for the home were created by the Maharams' son-in-law and daughter, David Pill and Hillary Maharam, who work as a team in their Pill-Maharam Architects firm, handling exteriors, interiors, and landscaping. The designers also credit the building contractor, Earle Zachau, for the

# THE *Maine* EVENT

Right: *Shadows are chased from the living room interiors by brilliant exterior light. The low-profile furnishings anchor the cathedral ceiling.*

Left: *By bringing a short wall of log ends into the living room, designers David Pill and Hillary Maharam created a stacked sculpture of sorts.*

Above: *From the second-floor landing, visitors can study the deceptive simplicity of the home's design.*

successful completion of the project.

"My father gave us the most basic criteria," Hillary says. "The house had to be made out of logs with a master bedroom upstairs and two bedrooms downstairs."

Constructed with honey-colored lodgepole pine on a stone foundation, the home blends well with the forest that wraps around the Maharams' house like a warm embrace. The cabin rises on a knoll, offering a view across 12-mile-long Sebago Lake, located 20 miles from Portland.

Though David and Hillary had never built with logs, they soon discovered the material's inherent strengths. Timbers make massive walls, which easily span cavernous rooms, and their soft tone and rugged texture invite inclusion of other natural building elements. For the Maine house, these include a fireplace of fieldstones salvaged from the old stacked-rock walls of New England, honed granite countertops, floors of 10-inch-wide pine planks, and a lead-coated copper roof.

"At first, my parents were worried that a metal roof would look too cold and would prove to be too expensive," says Hillary. "But we convinced them that this roofing material with a standing seam would lend just the right character when combined with the logs. And it does. Visually, it pulls the whole thing together."

But logs do make demands on builders. Chiefly, trees don't grow in uniform, standard sizes the way manufactured materials do. So, the builder and architect have to allow for variations in log size. Also, walls made from tree trunks often result in dark cabin interiors. It takes substantial

THE *Maine* EVENT

Right: *Gracing the dining room is an old French Canadian farm table with a muddy barn-red top.*

Left: *Part of the kitchen is slightly tucked away from the main living area so the cook can balance visiting and chores. The countertop is 1½-inch-thick Vermont granite.*

Above: *This 18-foot-square screened porch is attached to the entry wall of the cabin so those just arriving can find quick shelter from summer's mosquitoes.*

glass to brighten shadowy log cabin rooms.

"We decided to go with big windows and groups of windows so we could take full advantage of the lake view, fill rooms with plenty of light, and still allow for whole walls of log—so the cabin reads as a log structure when you see it," Hillary says.

Light also was brought into the upper story's master bedroom suite by opening it toward the lake with a broad shed dormer. Its height accommodates an 18-foot span of sliding glass doors. Not only do these doors give access to a secluded deck, but they also allow anyone reclining in bed to gaze out toward the vista of the lake and sky.

"You really feel like you are in a tree house," says Bonnie. "But even with the expanse of glass, it feels totally private."

For public occasions, the main level of the house offers entertaining space. Guests entering through the screened porch step into an unobstructed area encompassing living room, dining room, and kitchen. A pair of bedrooms and bathrooms are just a few steps down the hall.

To furnish such a pleasing home, the family has combined old and new pieces that are comfortable, sometimes amusing, and often handcrafted. Everywhere there are small treats for the body and soul: overstuffed chairs, antique birdhouses, Amish quilts, birchbark rockers, and whirligigs.

This skillfully created atmosphere is a world apart from the pressures of city life, and it brings joy full circle for Don.

As a boy, he experienced the manly adventure of camp. Now, as a man, he can taste again that boy's life. □

# THE *Maine* EVENT

OPEN TO LIVING / DINING

BALCONY

MASTER BEDROOM

DN

CLOS

BATH

UPPER LEVEL

SCREENED PORCH

LIVING

BEDROOM

BEDROOM

UP

HALL

DINING

KITCHEN

BATH

BATH

MAIN LEVEL

Left: *Rustic does not necessarily mean roughing it. This master bedroom suite includes a fully appointed bath and walk-in closet.*

Top: *The floor plan is simple and uncluttered.*

Right: *Clothes pegs in the guest bedroom were mounted on a board split from a log left after construction.*

Above: *Hillary Maharam and her husband, David Pill, work as a team doing architectural and landscape design.*

129

# Side by Side

*Working hand in glove, Brooks Garcia and his mother, Betty, have nurtured a wooded wonderland on this suburban lot.*

**BY LINDA JOAN SMITH. PRODUCED BY RUTH L. REITER**

The garden wraps around the shoulders of Betty Garcia's Atlanta ranch house like a velvet cloak, emerald in color and richly embroidered. Its meandering pathways are soft underfoot, its dense foliage bejeweled with moisture. Lush and sensuous, this shady bit of paradise is as well-cast for an elegant Victorian garden tea as for the moonlit revels of a midsummer night's dream.

It's the work of not one gardener but two, toiling side by side under the canopy of trees on the ¾-acre lot. Like most good teams, they've divided up the work.

"Brooks plants and I maintain the garden," says Betty Garcia, who has lived here for 19 years. "I cut the

Left: *The spring garden is lush with foxglove; campanula and blue and white violas peek forth from under their skirts.*
Above left: *Brooks Garcia learned to garden here at age 13; that early interest has blossomed into a passion for garden design.*
Above right: *Betty Garcia lovingly tends what Brooks plants.*

Photographs: Mary Carolyn Pindar

131

# Side by Side

grass, do the edging, pruning, and fertilizing, and work with Brooks when he comes over."

The partnership is long-lived; Brooks began working on the garden when he was in grammar school and a neighbor sparked his gardening interest. Now, at age 32, he's a professional garden designer who lives elsewhere in Atlanta but still returns to his mother's home to expand on his original work. "The garden was my way to experiment," says Brooks. "It's where I learned most of the things I know about gardening."

He's continued to experiment as the years have gone by. Betty's garden is now a lighthearted mix of formality and fun, divided into garden "rooms," each of which has a distinctive theme.

The spring garden at the front of the house, for instance, is based on a dignified four-cornered plan, yet it harbors rustic cedar chairs: the height of informality. Even the formal focal point—a treelike standard at the garden's center—was created from honeysuckle, a vine with decidedly unpretentious leanings.

From the spring garden, one can wander down a narrow garden along the flank of the house to the back,

---

Right: *Clematis arches over the entry to the woodland garden. Brooks rescued the gate from a nearby apartment complex undergoing demolition; the fence was scavenged from a dumpster. The color and choice of flowering vine were inspired by the work of famous English gardener Rosemary Verey.*
Top left: *Hostas, rosebud impatiens, and Boston fern fringe the side garden. Brooks salvaged the doors at both ends of the long space from a construction site, then built arbors to fit.*
Top right: *Like wood nymphs, statues peek from many garden spots. This one guards the fish pond at the head of the perennial border. Interlaced—or pleached—hornbeams, trained on poles and wire, form a leafy fence on the right.*

# Side by Side

where a stone fish pond, perennial border, long finger of lawn, and a woodland garden await. Each area has its bit of Brooks's magic: a gazing sphere that reflects the branches overhead, an iron gate painted a startling purple-blue, a birdbath with an island of glass, a statue that beckons from a shadowed bower. Architectural elements are scattered through the garden; many are salvaged finds—straw turned to gold by Brooks's touch.

"People need to do gardens that are expressions of themselves," Brooks says, "not a copy of some other garden type." He advises beginners to dig in and let the garden do the teaching. He tells the story of a woman who came time and again to the nursery where he worked, but she never bought plants. "I asked her why, and she said she didn't know enough yet." He shakes his head. "You've got to get out there and start—just do it. You'll make some mistakes, but you can always dig it up, pull it, move it, try something different."

Betty lets Brooks have free rein over most of the garden design and is quite content to nurture what he's planted. But where there is teamwork, there's inevitably a need for compromise. There are plans in the works for a roadside garden, a sunnier spot than the rest. "Mother wants irises, snapdragons, and hollyhocks. I want more roses," says Brooks. All will likely flourish. □

*Right: Pineapple garden ornaments from Italy, perched atop mortarless pedestals of brick, welcome visitors to the spring garden, now in its fourth year of growth.*
*Top left: The gazing sphere, a gift from a friend, is surrounded by a collection of Bonica and Fairy roses, pansies, erigeron, and silene, the latter grown from seeds Brooks collected in France.*
*Top right: The birdbath, backed by an oak-leaf hydrangea and surrounded by helleborus, was Brooks's grandfather's; the path beyond the cedar arbor leads to the woodland garden.*

*In the converted barn behind her historic Connecticut home, furniture designer, author, and former magazine editor JoAnn Barwick celebrates summer with her grandchildren, who anticipate "Camp JoAnn" from one year to the next.*

# Camp JoAnn

T he girls don't care a whit that their camp director pioneered country design in the 1970s, contributing to a new mindset on how people live. Or that, in effect, she imported Scandinavian country style into American homes in the '80s, again changing the lives of many. Nor are they much impressed by her redoubtable stature as a veteran decorating pundit whose nod can breathe life into an emerging design trend—or whose shrug can chop it off at the knees.

The only real homage they pay her professional achievements is essentially self-indulgent: Sprawled on the Weekend Retreat furnishings she designed for Lexington Furniture Industries, and which decorate their camp "headquarters," they richly enjoy the fruits of her labor. No one needs to tell them the furniture collection was designed in the informal language of summer home living to provide kicked-back comfort and spur both nostalgia and a platoon of good times for future memories. These kids get it.

The kids are the granddaughters and grandnieces of JoAnn Barwick, former editor of *House Beautiful,* founding editor of *Country Living,* author of *Scandinavian Country,* and, most recently, a design consultant and spokesperson for Lexington and other Masco Corp. companies. In the restored barn behind JoAnn's 18th-century home in New Preston, Connecticut, the girls descend every

---

BY CANDACE ORD MANROE

⚜

Left: *The 150-year-old barn of JoAnn Barwick and husband, Fred Berger, was moved from Vermont to Connecticut.*
Opposite, top left: *JoAnn uses the barn behind her home as her office when it's not camp season.*
Below: *JoAnn's family revels in camp.*

Photographs: Children's portrait, William Bennett Seitz; others, Langdon Clay

137

summer to spend one week of organized fun honing their skills at art, drama, swimming, fishing, cooking, music, and dance.

The camp director is, of course, JoAnn. Camp JoAnn is a sobriquet bestowed by the campers themselves. Taking their lead, JoAnn even had T-shirts printed with the camp name for each of the children.

More than an opportunity for enrichment, the camp's real purpose is to draw the family together.

"The reason I started this camp was so that my grandchildren, who live in South Hampton, could get to know their cousins from Vermont. It's also an excuse for me to be camp counselor," admits JoAnn. "I can take a walk with the girls and say all the things I want to share with them and have them listen, because I'm the camp director."

JoAnn's husband, Fred Berger, is the official camp chef and instructor of the girls' cooking classes. (When camp is out, Fred resumes his career

as a public relations consultant for travel and health care companies.) Swimming classes in the pool behind the barn are a daily camp event, but that's about the only constant. With JoAnn planning the itinerary, each day is jammed with opportunities for creativity in a variety of media.

Recalling last summer's camp, JoAnn says, "One day it was a hat-making class, using dried flowers at a decorator's home. Another day it was working with a well-known potter, closing their eyes and feeling the clay, then making face masks, which we presented to the girls on their last night."

⚜

*Left and* above: *Outfitted entirely in JoAnn's Weekend Retreat collection for Lexington Furniture Industries, the barn's sleeping porch is a central hang-out for JoAnn's campers. Here they bunk overnight and rest between work-outs in the pool, just out the door.*

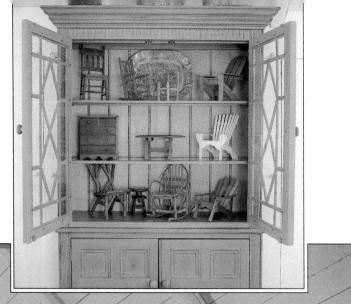

Below: *Wearing contemporary whitewash, the barn's main upstairs room is for living, dining, and sleeping. JoAnn had the barn in mind when she conceived the Weekend Retreat line that furnishes it.*
Right: *The Nantucket cabinet hosts JoAnn's cache of miniature furniture.*

❧

*Right: JoAnn's thinking in designing Weekend Retreat was to create furniture that looked as if it had been painted and recycled for a summer house—thus the collection's "Light Cottage Green" shutter headboard and the white bedside commode.*

*Below right: The Lighthouse lamp table also features a recycled look in its "Light Cottage Green" finish.*

Last summer's balanced regimen of camp events also included a day of sporting activities during which JoAnn's son took the girls on a fishing expedition to a river where they camped overnight.

Another day, an art teacher visited the girls back at Camp JoAnn, mixing the discipline of painting with music and dance.

"First, she played classical music while they painted," JoAnn recalls. "Then she played a ballet, brought out large scarves, and they danced with scarves. Then she put on rock music, and with no prodding from us, they began to paint their bodies. Watching this creative energy come out of them, I was stunned."

But that was only the beginning. The real measure of the girls' capacity for absorbing and releasing creative impulses came at the end-of-camp awards banquet.

Adults planned the banquet, complete with a bonfire to set the proper out-in-the-woods mood. But the campers spent all the week before the event secretly preparing a program of their own.

On banquet night, the girls treated the adults to an elaborate show replete with drama, song, dance, and costumes. "The two girls who take jazz dancing lessons were the choreographers," says JoAnn.

As the backdrop for the high-energy week's worth of Camp JoAnn, the barn is a natural. Nothing's too precious here for even the most rambunctious moments of creativity and spontaneity. The girls bunk on kid-size Murphy beds that pull out from the wall of the sleeping porch. Virtually all other furniture in the barn, both on the sleeping porch and in the main living quarters upstairs, is JoAnn's Weekend Retreat collection for Lexington.

The appropriateness of the Weekend Retreat pieces for the barn, kids, and camp is not a matter of happenstance. "I must've been thinking about this barn when I was designing the collection," says JoAnn. "I didn't know it at the time, but looking back, everything I

Left: *Used as a guesthouse when camp is out, the barn includes a well-stocked kitchen.*

Below: *JoAnn's white Harbour House table and Old Sweden chairs reflect her Scandinavian heritage with their gentle blue and white.*

wanted to accomplish in the furniture collection relates to the feelings I have about the barn."

JoAnn restored the barn, which had been moved from Vermont, to serve as an airy counterpoint to her 18th-century home's darker rooms.

"I love the barn's combination of simplicity and serenity. As a barn, it's a casual space, but it's whitewashed and filled with light, becoming very contemporary. It's my hideaway—my refuge from the daily routine, where I can escape to read a book," she explains.

JoAnn wanted her Weekend Retreat furnishings to have a similarly uplifting, refreshing effect. "The whole idea behind Weekend Retreat was to remind you of wonderful summer or getaway places that you've loved," she says.

"There's nothing startling about any of the pieces. They're intentionally familiar," she adds. "I used the soothing colors of water and summer green to suggest relaxation and comfort. None of the pieces are serious—no important mahoganies. Instead, there's the look of well-worn pine or a painted blue that suggests gener-

ations of caring, perhaps having started out as a serious piece but having been painted for use in a summer cottage."

Like her summer camp for kids, JoAnn's furniture is all about rekindling the heart. "Weekend Retreat is an invitation for more people to rethink their lives," she says. "We can surround ourselves with the people and the things that make us feel good. It's OK to give ourselves an emotional reward."

# October

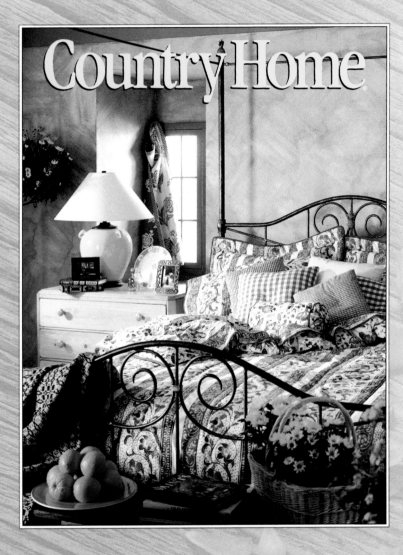

# In Harmony With the Earth

*The Southwestern spirit of a Santa Fe adobe appeals to Robert Nichols' lifelong passion for Native American arts and ways.*

Right: *Adobe homes seem to emerge whole from the earth.*

Below: *Robert Nichols surrounds himself with Indian pottery.*

Right: *By choosing pieces such as the handsomely carved, 19th-century writing desk made in New York, Robert steers clear of Southwestern furnishing clichés.*

L ike the early-1900s adobe house in which he has long resided, the life of Robert Nichols is rooted in the sandy, baked soil of the great American Southwest.

Robert was born in Arizona and launched his professional life more than 30 years ago, exploring the fragile ruins of the Anasazi Indian cliff dwellings at Mesa Verde in southern Colorado's desert.

There, amid broken shards of clay pottery dating back nearly 1,000 years, Robert found his future. He would work for the next 20 years as an anthropologist and ranger with the National Park Service. He helped plan exhibits

**BY STEVE COOPER**
**PRODUCED BY MARY ANNE THOMSON**

Photographs: William N. Hopkins, Hopkins Associates

# In Harmony With the Earth

Although at first glance Pueblo Indian pottery, left, appears confined to a narrow band of form and color, on closer inspection a subtle variety emerges. Each pueblo has its own artistic signature, which is seen in the choices of shadings and images. Robert's collection, displayed in the 1820s Pennsylvania cupboard, includes the white-clay bowls of the Acoma, the yellowware of the Hopi, and red pottery of the Zia.

explaining Native American history and culture at parks throughout the country. Then, in 1980, he established a Santa Fe, New Mexico, gallery specializing in Indian pottery.

It seems appropriate that a man with such a deep appreciation for Indian culture should live in a house whose design derives from ancient building techniques indigenous to this arid region. Since pre-Columbian times, peoples of the Southwest have fashioned walls from adobe—sun-dried bricks formed from the clay-rich soil found here.

Robert was drawn to his particular adobe farmhouse because its rooms are filled with an unusual amount of light during the day.

"Many adobes are dark, but this one has never been like that. What I really find appealing about this house is the extraordinary quality of light inside," he says.

Interiors have another out-of-the-ordinary feature. They weren't furnished to be just another one-note update of the Old West style. Instead, Robert's rooms are home to such divergent antiques as English Arts and Crafts furniture, a 19th-century

Empire chest, hooked rugs from Virginia, a Shaker bonnet, homespun linens, a stack of cowboy hats, and, of course, a display of fine antique and contemporary Indian pottery.

Robert says, "I'm very pleased with the broad mixture of antiques and objects in my home. Since I enjoy

*R*obert *reached far beyond New Mexico to gather an eclectic assortment of living room furnishings,* above. *It took a skillful eye to include English Arts and Crafts chairs, an old Santa Fe church candelabra, and an 1880s Chippendale chest. The two hooked rugs,* opposite, *with their folk art depictions of chickens and cats were both made by hand on the East Coast around the turn of the century.*

*W*armed by sunlight,
the dining room, left,
has a sturdy and sparse
Western elegance.

*In the dining room
corner, a cupboard from
Pennsylvania solves a
problem common to
homes built in the early
1900s: There are few
closets or cabinets for
the storage of linens,
flatware, and dishes.*

Indian pottery and more traditional American pottery, why not have them both? I like a variety, and many other people do, too."

This delightful diversity was created with the help of interior designer Jonathan Parks. His furnishing selections underscore the enchanting variation seen in New Mexico's ever-changing landscape.

"You see so much color here," says Jonathan, "the basic earth tones, the soothing sky, the mountains. You don't want to compete with nature—you want to fit in. So you find things that feel like they belong."

With this criteria, materials and hues became the measure by which pieces were chosen. It didn't matter so much when a certain chair was made or what style it was, as it did that all furnishings felt right for inclusion in Robert's adobe.

The result is a house with style in Santa Fe, rather than a Santa Fe-style house. It's eclectic without a hint of oddity or eccentricity.

This refreshing blend of styles and designs is evident throughout the house, but is best seen in the living room. Here, carved Hispanic figures stand on a Chippendale chest dating to the 1880s, a Shaker-style clock in a red

buttermilk paint graces one wall, and an Eastern cupboard filled with Indian pottery stands along an opposing wall.

Even with his Indian pottery, Robert refuses to be hemmed in by artificial constraints concerning style. While some collectors limit their selections to the work of a particular pueblo, a single family, or a certain artist, Robert is a firm believer in diversity.

"I've always been more concerned about the individual piece—its form, the quality of the decoration, how it works with my other pottery," he says, "rather than being only concerned about it coming from a certain family or time period."

He encourages other less-seasoned collectors to follow their own instincts and passions. Robert sees too many customers who are timid when deciding their purchases.

"My approach to choosing pottery—and this can be applied to any kind of collection—has always been very personal and unabashedly emotional," he says. "I think it's OK for one to like whatever one likes. I also think that anyone who relies too much on advice from someone else, whether an expert or a friend, is missing out on one of the great joys of collecting: passion."

But how is an intense commitment

*T*he Indian shield above Robert's bed, above right, *inspires dreams of buffalo hunts,
campfires, and bravery. Also hanging above his bed is one of the home's many hooked
rugs. Designer Jonathan Parks says, "Textiles are like art painted by a weaver."
A small herd of carved horses,* opposite, *was corralled atop the bedroom's Empire chest.
The bowlegged, lasso-twirlin', chaps-wearin' cowpoke was whittled in the 1920s.*

# In
# Harmony
### With the
# Earth

*Beginning with neutral white walls, right, Jonathan Parks brought sky and earth colors into the bedroom with three 1920s rugs above the bed, a distinctive cherry-wood wardrobe, and blue-and-white homespun shams. He topped it all off with a stack of cowboy hats.*

to the gathering of objects developed? For Robert, it all goes back to long, hot days sifting through the remnants of a vanished culture as he explored the Anasazi ruins.

Robert says, "I spent two years

analyzing many of the ten thousand pieces of pottery we found at the cliff dwellings. An experience like that becomes the focus of both a person's work and pursuits."

It even influenced his decision to buy his two-bedroom adobe. The home's earthy architecture conjured just the right images of Indian pueblos rising on desert plateaus.

But Robert's house was actually built in two sections, and only the older portion is true adobe-brick construction. This part, now a small kitchen and dining room, was erected around 1900.

The rest of the two-bedroom home was added in the 1930s. Although it also appears to be adobe, this side merely mimics the earthen facade.

Builders did this by framing walls so they were nearly a foot thick—similar to the stocky appearance of adobe structures. Then the walls were coated with sand-colored plaster. The results perfectly match the older, authentic-adobe portion of the house.

"It's quite a seamless job. You can't tell where they joined the two halves of the house," Robert says.

So all is harmonious. Robert's house is an effortless blending of his love for the Southwest, Americana, Indian culture, and the earth. □

# BEYOND
## *The Beaten*
# PATH

*Deep in the Long Island woods, Cris and Mike Spindler's
farm is alive with wildlife, hard-to-find plants,
and visitors who linger to drink in the peace and quiet.*

Passersby seduced by the sign for the
Peconic River Herb Farm are in for a
surprise. Once they brave the rutted
dirt drive, visitors find themselves in a
wooded oasis that is one part nursery,
one part homestead, and one part
wildlife refuge. A quick stop to buy a
5-inch pot of lemon thyme often
stretches into an afternoon spent
wandering in the woods, soaking up
sunlight and birdsong, and delighting
in the scents of a thousand blooms.

Indigo buntings—the males a
startling azure hue—flit among the
brambles. Deer peek timidly from amid
stands of oaks, and muskrats glide in
silence along the muddy banks of the
Peconic. Along with the natural flora
and fauna, there are 22 gardens to

BY LINDA JOAN SMITH
PRODUCED BY BONNIE MAHARAM

Photographs at Peconic River Herb Farm: William Stites

Opposite: *Cris Spindler began the Peconic River Herb Farm seven years ago, with help from her husband, Mike. Mike has since built the property's two barns, numerous raised beds, and four greenhouses. Sons Luke, 13, and Seth, 7, often lend a hand.*

Left: *A leafy tepee made of metal reinforcing rods and morning-glories shelters a table in the children's garden.*

Below: *Columbine thrive in the woodland shade.*

Right: *Perennial borders, chairs, and picnic tables scattered about the farm welcome city visitors who are tired of congestion and eager for calm. This bed is lush with foxglove, coralbells, veronica, and pink clusters of meadow rue.*

Opposite: *The garden's floral and herbal produce.*

Below, from left: *Forget-me-not, basil, and thyme are among the plants Cris sells.*

explore: a children's garden, butterfly garden, woodland garden, thyme garden, fragrance garden, and more.

The farm's evolution was as organic as the trillium that sprout and thrive in cool glades among the trees. Returning from a canoe trip on the Peconic River 12 years ago, Cris and Mike spotted a "For Sale" sign in the woods along the road. "We were only twenty-one, and not really looking for property," says Cris. When the advertised 7 acres turned out to be 13, with waterfront on their favorite canoeing river, Cris says, they "went crazy. We had to have it."

The property was densely wooded; Cris and Mike cleared trees and brush by hand for two years before there was room to build a house. Soon after, they moved themselves and 3-year-old son Luke into a rustic 20-by-24-foot log cabin, which they built after consulting books in the local library.

With a second child on the way, Cris decided to start "some sort of small farm venture" so she could work from home. A horticulture class provided the groundwork, and in May 1986 Cris opened the Peconic River Herb Farm, just as interest in herb gardening and cooking was on the rise.

Along with an array of herbs, she featured hard-to-find plants such as

heirloom vegetable and flower varieties, flowers and shrubs that attract butterflies and birds, and plants native to Long Island. "We're very off the beaten path," says Cris. "But people started coming down almost every day. One car, two cars—it was really exciting." Now, even with four greenhouses for starting plants, Cris can barely keep up with the demand.

Though Cris is always on the run, she advises customers, particularly new gardeners, simply to relax.

"People come down here and they've read too many garden books that tell them all these dos and don'ts," she says. "But you're not planting this permanent thing. You can move perennials around. Just experiment and enjoy yourself."

Her enthusiasm is contagious. Many of Cris's customers find themselves toting home her favorite plants, such as species clematis, or one of the 40 different scented geraniums she grows.

Most of all, visitors to the Peconic River Herb Farm take home a taste of serenity. The sweet scent of chocolate cosmos. The cool breath of the deep woods. The sharp whistle of an osprey as it hovers over the river. And the sense of having stepped, for a moment, well beyond the beaten path. □

*Through this portal of peace and tranquillity lies the stylish, romantic Colorado hideaway of Bill and Karla Walsh.*

By Steve Cooper
Produced By Linda Joan Smith
And Mindy Pantiel

# Refined Retreat

# Refined Retreat

For five years now, Bill and Karla Walsh have been leading a double life.

Three weeks a month during most of the year, the couple lives the contemporary condominium life in Wichita, Kansas. Bill has a full plate of responsibilities as a restaurateur, and Karla regularly works as a volunteer at an emergency care shelter for abandoned and abused children.

But the demands take their toll, and the Walshes enjoy taking frequent breaks. They know if they don't escape, the routines of Wichita would become an all-too-familiar drill.

So, the couple regularly loads up the car and heads out for their refined Rocky Mountain retreat—a spacious, Colorado cabin.

"When I think of the one place on earth I'd like to be, it's the cabin. It's the most serene and most beautiful place I know of," Karla says.

A rustic mood is evoked by the massive golden logs

Opposite: *Antique bent willow rockers stand sentry at the front door.*

Top: *Open eaves give the cabin a chalet-like feel.*

Above: *Karla and Bill Walsh are joined by their chocolate Labrador, Chelsea, for a relaxed family portrait.*

stacked to form the cabin's walls. But this isn't the rustic of Colorado's buckaroo days. This is today's West, where every designer seems to have a line of signature cowboy hats, fortune hunters seek their gold in jewelry stores, and cabins are no longer the cobbled-together shacks of miners, cowpokes, and homesteading pioneers.

The Walshes' snug condo is dwarfed by their second home in Keystone. The two homes are as different as a narrow canyon and the open prairie.

Designed by architect Peter Witter's firm (now in Santa Rosa, California), the house can accommodate a whole crew of friends or family. There are four bedrooms, and the dining room is large enough to seat 10 guests. When the living room is overflowing with visitors, parties can easily move outside onto a pair of expansive decks.

Interiors have been invested with a timeless character. Many of the

Photographs: William N. Hopkins, Hopkins Associates; homeowner portrait, Todd Powell

chairs, tables, and cabinets are antique pieces, and those that aren't have been chosen because they exude a quality of old-fashioned craftsmanship. These include a pine table from Ireland, English stained-glass windows mounted at the top of the stairwell, antique plumbing fixtures, and a salvaged hardwood cabinet used as an island in the kitchen.

The most dramatic find for the house was made by one of the cabin builders—a log left largely in its natural state with branches, curves, and twists intact. It stands as a stylish reminder that this is, after all, a Colorado retreat. The sweeping spruce tree with its limbs reaching to the ceiling now serves as an eye-catching, upright support in the home's foyer.

"The builders couldn't believe I wanted it," Karla says. "But it looks wonderful, and it always surprises people when they first come in the house."

Left: *To keep the living room from seeming cavernous, interior designer Julie Nicholson arranged overstuffed furnishings in a warm, intimate grouping.*

Top: *Another way to scale down a large space is by creating a private corner, such as this reading spot in the living room.*

Above: *The entry gains an unusual column when a tree trunk is left au naturel.*

Creating such a pleasing hideaway took plenty of planning and hard work, of course. But almost from the outset, the Walshes knew what they wanted. They bought their parcel of paradise in 1987, and the next day signed a contract for the logs.

"We hadn't yet even designed the house, and there we were making a commitment for the logs," Bill says. "I look back on decisions like that, and it amazes me that everything worked out. But it has and with hardly a hitch."

What prompted the impulse buy? Bill was hooked on his first visit to the log company's yard when the owner encouraged Bill to try his hand at a logger's skill—skinning loose bark with a drawknife. A few minutes of firsthand experience with the fallen spruce tree and Bill was smitten with log cabin fever.

"I fell in love with the whole concept of building a house from all of these

# Refined Retreat

incredible trees," he says.

Harvested locally, the logs are from 16 to 30 inches in diameter; the longest is about 48 feet. Rocks used for the foundation, partial walls, and fireplace also were gathered from the area.

But not everything about the house is pure Colorado. The Walshes scoured antique and architectural salvage shops in Nebraska, Kansas, and the Adirondack region of New York looking for unusual panel doors, furnishings, and fixtures that would give the cabin its zest.

Joining the couple on their treasure hunt was interior designer Julie Nicholson, who lived at the time in Wichita but has since moved her business to Memphis.

Karla says, "Even though I majored in interior decorating in college, I didn't have the confidence or the resources that someone who is in the business would have. So we

Above: *A log doorway leads to Karla's vanity table.*

Top: *Karla found a resting place for this 1930s spindle-and-sunburst bed in the cabin's guest bedroom. She chanced upon it in a Wichita shop.*

Left: *Escaping to the master bedroom, Bill or Karla can take care of correspondence at the leather armchair and fine old desk.*

Preceding pages: *The kitchen floor is knotty, soft pine.*

hired Julie to help pull the interiors together."

The best source they discovered was a now-closed wrecking company in Lincoln, Nebraska. It was a huge recycling center with stacks of dismantled house parts, such as doors, windows, mantels, sinks, tubs, and other relics.

Bill, Karla, and Julie had the misfortune of sifting through the hoard on the coldest day of the year. "We rummaged through this barn picking out doors, and it was freezing cold," Bill says. "But we found twenty-eight doors that we were able to use in our house."

Their favorite was a five-panel, round-top door. It so impressed the architect, he designed an opening just for this antique.

"Most new houses look new," Julie says. "But the wonderful thing about using logs and the salvaged doors we found is that they give a place an instant patina.

# Refined Retreat

The house looks as though it's been sitting there forever."

With such an enticing retreat beckoning, Karla admits it's increasingly difficult to return to the Wichita condominium after a Colorado visit. The day will come when the couple will call Colorado their home, she says.

"I already live here full-time through the summer months, though Bill can't do that yet," Karla says. "It's just a matter of time before we can both live at the cabin year-round."

In the meantime, the house is big enough for Bill to host occasional extended business meetings here or have family members in for summer stays. During one vacation week, the house was filled with 27 parents, siblings, aunts, uncles, and cousins.

"The oven was going twenty-four hours a day. We pitched tents on the deck for the kids, and everyone had a great time," Karla says.

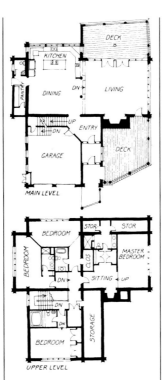

Top: *An Irish dining table accommodates 10 people.*

Above: *According to plan, each upstairs bedroom has its own bath.*

There are also smaller gatherings with just one or two older relatives.

"I feel very fortunate to have a place to bring aunts and uncles who are in their sixties or seventies," she says. "It's really thrilling to get to know them at this point in our lives. It's been a benefit of owning the cabin that I never really anticipated."

Another benefit for the Walshes is having the golden spruce, the glowing fireplace, and the sunny decks all to themselves. There's also a cozy eating spot for two in the kitchen.

"The little table is really our favorite place in the house," Karla says. "You can sit quietly and look out at the forest. We like to take a long time there for breakfast and talk."

But are the view and the quiet the only attractions? No, it's also romantic.

She adds, "But, then, that's what makes our cabin special. It's a very romantic place." □

# December

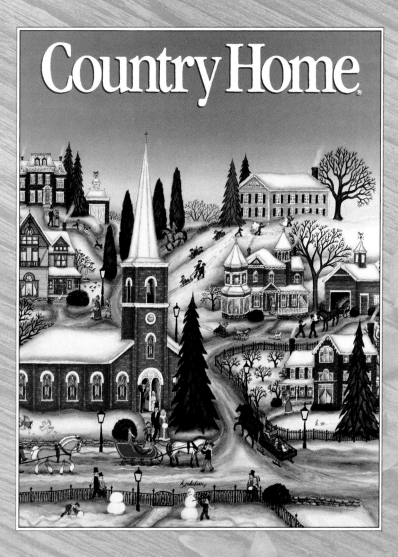

# *Reflections*
## OF DECEMBERS PAST

*For more than 200 years, families have been celebrating the season in the Connecticut home of Roberta and Mark Velez.*

BY STEVE COOPER. PRODUCED BY JOSEPH BOEHM

Opposite: *The angel hovering atop the living room Christmas tree was a gift from Roberta Velez's mother.*
Top: *Candles are displayed in each of the home's 23 windows.*
Above: *Roberta and Mark Velez in their 18th-century best.*

It can't be said with any historical accuracy that families of early American colonists once gathered around the Christmas goose at the Connecticut home that now belongs to Roberta and Mark Velez.

But isn't it fun to think it might be true?

About 20 years before the Revolution, Christ's birth may have been toasted in the same rooms where Roberta and Mark now embrace the year's special day with friends and family.

Though there may be gaps in the Velezes' knowledge of their home's history, they have discovered much since purchasing the farmhouse in the town of Griswold eight years ago. They have invested long hours of detective work tracing deeds and other early documents.

The couple says they believe the initial building was erected as early as the winter of 1757 by Lemuel Withy, or McWeth, or a similar name. Mark has documented 31 spellings of the family's name so far and cannot say with absolute certainty which spelling was used at that particular time. Reconfiguring history is rather like unscrambling an egg.

"The date I gave is my best guess," Mark says. "From the style of the architecture, it may actually prove to be older. But if I make an error, I'd much rather err with a more conservative estimate."

Inspired by their home's historical setting, the couple

167

# Reflections

*Left: The fireplace and rich fabrics warm the keeping room. Roberta made the family stockings from Oriental rugs. Her favorite stuffer? A diamond and amethyst ring from Mark. Above: Those aren't gingerbread men on the taproom tree. They are made from cinnamon and applesauce.*

celebrates a colonial-style holiday. They even dress for the occasion in 18th-century costumes, and guests often join the fun by donning powdered wigs and tricornered hats from the Velezes' wardrobe collection. In this home, Christmas and history are playfully mixed.

"There's a wonderful mystique to this house at Christmas when the fireplaces are going and all of our guests have joined us," Roberta says. "It's like no other place I've lived."

As many as 25 people join in the revelry each year. The day's meal begins with shrimp and antipasto at 1 p.m. sharp and winds its leisurely way toward the bounteous main courses, including ham, turkey, and a lasagna made by Roberta's mother, Annette Ceruzzi. Serving dinner takes from 3 to 7 p.m. Then there are the desserts. John Maratea, the baker in the family, brings his special braided breads and pies.

A highlight of each celebration is Mark's annual batch of artillery punch. Victorious patriots lifted mugs of this potent concoction—a mix of tea, champagne, wine, juice, and spirits—to the Revolution. For Roberta, the punch is another small way of maintaining continuity with her home's past. Because history seems present and real, it's almost as if unseen companions join the toasts.

Roberta says, "The joy of living in a house this old is imagining all the events and all the visitors that might have come into the rooms where you now live. You can

almost feel their presence in the house."

Mark feels equally strong about having a home with a past.

"Newer houses don't have a soul," he says.

The Colonial house reflects the age in which it was built. It is a sturdy commoner with no use for pretentious adornment, as its beauty and function are inseparably woven together. The architectural lines are strong, straight, and sure. The clapboard siding couldn't be more utilitarian, but it is still graceful. Window and door treatments are appropriately restrained yet handsome.

As often occurred in colonial times, the home was built in two sections. The oldest has four fireplaces, including one built for cooking. It appears there might have been much reason to cook.

"We have found documentation showing that this was a pork farm selling food to the army during the

## Reflections

Above: *Before the Velezes bought the home, Roberta began collecting 19th-century china in anticipation of owning a historical house.*
Opposite: *Much of the dining room paneling had to be replaced.*
Below: *Fireplaces are central to the Velez home's floor plan.*

Revolution," Roberta says. "When I stand in the keeping room, sometimes I wonder whether they were planning raids in this house during the war. It makes me feel more like a caretaker than a homeowner."

Caretaker is the right word because the house has demanded quite a bit of attention. Among problems that were fixed:

• A new red cedar roof was applied.

• Fresh courses of quarter-sawn clapboard siding were anchored with hand-forged nails.

• Granite and brick chimneys were enlarged.

• New windows sashes also were installed.

Because of the long list of needed renovations, Mark was reluctant to buy. He and Roberta had once restored a Victorian-era residence, but this place was a disaster.

On the other hand, the house was just the relic of

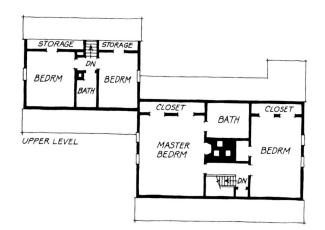

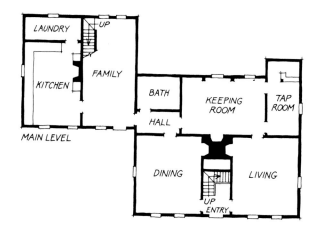

Floor plan illustrations: Carson Ode

# *Reflections*

Left: *For longer than the United States has been a nation, fires and Christmas have cheered residents of this house.*
Above: *The teddy bear in the guest bedroom is Mark's, who has had it since he was a baby. It sits on a side chair that dates to the late 18th century.*

history Roberta had dreamt about since her youth.

"Ever since I was a twelve-year-old girl, I've wanted a house like this," she says.

And in the end, of course, she got her wish.

"The house won me over," Mark says. "It has so much character to it. It's not at all like a modern house."

The atmosphere today is authentically early American. One room has rough-hewn open beams; beams in another room have been boxed in a traditionally colonial manner. The floors have been made from pine, oak, butternut, and chestnut. Fireplaces and their well-worn surrounds look their age.

Bringing the home back to its present condition was a five-year project. The Velezes even had a live-in carpenter for nine months during the restoration.

"Until you've attempted something like this, you have no idea how much work and effort it will take. I still can't believe we did it," Roberta says.

In the couple of years since major renovations have been completed, the Velezes have reveled in their role as the home's temporary caretakers.

Roberta says, "I guess it's what I said before: It has a mystique. What could be better than living in a true piece of Americana at Christmastime?" ■

# Woodland Dreaming

Left: *During Christmas, Jean LemMon shares her Norwegian heritage and family traditions with her daughter and son-in-law, Becky and Bill Matykowski. Below and following details: Jean's antique and heirloom ornaments are a sparkling legacy.*

*For years, Jean LemMon had driven by the Cape Cod cottage tucked into the woods in a quiet neighborhood in Des Moines, Iowa, and dreamed of making it her own. In time for Christmas last year, her wish came true.*

**BY CANDACE ORD MANROE**
**PRODUCED WITH JOSEPH BOEHM AND PEGGY A. FISHER**

Photographs: Interiors, William N. Hopkins, Hopkins Associates; Jean's antique ornaments, Perry Struse; exterior, Jean LemMon

175

# Woodland Dreaming

*Opposite: Each Christmas Eve, a cheery fire and candles greet Jean's church friends who drop in for a buffet. Left: Jean's Scandinavian offerings include jam-filled sandbakkels, ice-cream-cone-like krumkakke, and kranskakke (a wreath cake that is eaten from the bottom up).*

Jean recognized the house from her dreams: The light-saturated, crisp yet serene spaces unfolded, room by room, just as they had night after night in her sleep. Seeing the real house on its shaded street at the edge of a park, she knew exactly how it would feel to wake up in its second-story bedroom, beneath a canopy of trees and lacy sunlight. Each time she drove by the house, the dream became more real.

Jean's background—serving as editor-in-chief of *Country Home*® magazine for seven years before leaving in May to head its larger sister publication, *Better Homes and Gardens*®—helped her pursue her dream. The years of working around the best examples of interior design had taught her exactly what she wanted in a home, and this house had it all. So, to those who know her, it came as no shock last fall when Jean made an offer on the house at the first glimmer of a For Sale sign.

Desiring to usher in a snowy Christmas Eve before the home's hearth, Jean acted with alacrity, buying the house

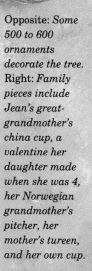

Opposite: *Some 500 to 600 ornaments decorate the tree.* Right: *Family pieces include Jean's great-grandmother's china cup, a valentine her daughter made when she was 4, her Norwegian grandmother's pitcher, her mother's tureen, and her own cup.*

before even thinking of selling her old one.

"It was a risk, because I'm not independently wealthy," she admits. "But the bigger risk was to let this house slip away."

Celebrating the holidays in her new home was everything Jean had anticipated. Soft drifts of snow arrived on cue, and chains of icicles—nature's own tinsel—glittered at the windows. Only the small hoofprints of deer interrupted the placid sea of white surrounding the house.

Jean decorated the cottage for the holidays with an emphasis on heart and heritage, using natural greens and favorite family collectibles. She festooned boughs across the fireplace, windows, and canopy bed, filling spaces with the rich aroma of fir.

"I like to keep holiday decorating natural and simple," she says. "It's a carryover from the country Christmases I knew as a child, combined with the fact that I get claustrophobic surrounded by lots of glittery doodads, even at the holidays."

The special festive touches are compatible with the home's year-round appearance. "Being around design every day on the job, I'm most comfortable living with an 'undecorated' look," says Jean. "And nothing can compete with these views."

Beginning with trimming a live green tree, Jean shares some traditions year to year with her daughter and son-in-law, Becky and Bill Matykowski. Colorful bubble lights, popular in

# Woodland Dreaming

Right: *Jean's master bedroom commands treetop views. For Christmas, it's even more romantic with the canopy bed ribboned and garlanded with greens. Jean sponged the walls herself and hung old, simple but beautiful, crocheted panels at the windows.* Left: *Serene still lifes characterize the bedroom.*

postwar America but hard to find today, are called into active duty, along with 500 to 600 heirloom ornaments that are "carefully hung—nothing helter-skelter," says Jean.

"Although I'm not basically a persnickety person, I have always been fussy about how my Christmas tree looks. Thank heavens that Becky has always had a good design eye and, even as a kid, she did a creditable job of decorating the tree."

Scandinavian customs first learned during Jean's childhood in Duluth, Minnesota, also are observed, "including making lutefisk, which I always prepare but am the only one to eat," she says, laughing.

Another tradition Jean observes is to make sure she changes the chimes in her grandfather's clock so they ring like bells on Christmas Eve at dusk. "This is in observance of the Norwegian custom of the bells ringing in the villages on Christmas Eve," she says.

From the sanctuary of the snowy cottage in the woods, the clock bells evoke an old-world mood that's a perfect fit for the storybook setting of Jean's dreams. ■

# Yuletide Echoes

From their eclectic home in the canyons outside
Los Angeles, the Joneses ring in the holidays in cheery
style. Preparations include trimming live trees in
every room and dusting off the Christmas collectibles.

BY CANDACE ORD MANROE

**Left:** *For Christmas, Debra Jones replaces summery slipcovers on the living room sofas with a richer, leaf-green velvet. Her eclectic style includes curtains from a former house; antique fabrics on the wing chairs; and a lamp made from a watering can.*

✳

# Yuletide Echoes

**D**ebra Jones indulges three healthy obsessions: houses, collecting, and Christmas. Come December, they converge into a single passion to ready the home for the holidays—a pursuit shared by her 11-year-old daughter, Shannon, and abided by her husband, Parker.

"Christmas has always been a big deal in my family," explains Debra. "One night, we decorate our house; another night, my sister's; and another, my mother's guest house, which is on our property. We decorate right up to the last minute. My husband is tolerant of it, as my [late] father was, and as my new brother-in-law is."

The Joneses' home in the canyons outside Los Angeles is a natural for the green shades of Christmas. From its hillside perch, the house commands wooded vistas in every direction, without a single man-made structure impairing the views. Thanks to the home's ample windows, green becomes a part of the indoor living environment as well. "Everywhere you look you see only large trees," says Parker.

Plus, green happens to be Debra's favorite color. It's a decorating staple throughout the home year-round—and a bonus at Christmas.

"There's a lot of green in the home because I love it," admits Debra. "At Christmas, there's even more of it. I replace the summer white or green linen slipcovers on the living room couch with dark, leaf-green velvet slipcovers."

Dark green boat paint dramatizes the kitchen floor, and even the old tile floors in the laundry room and on the back porch feature a checkerboard pattern in snappy green and black.

Green dominates the entry as rich, glazed color on the walls. For Christmas, all that's needed is the tree. "We have a tree in every room

Right: A *mix of*
accessories that
includes old
bedspreads as
swag curtains,
vintage fabrics
on the chairs,
and folk art
makes the
family room the
coziest place in
the house.

Below, from
left: *Parker,
Shannon, and
Debra Jones.*

✳

# Yuletide Echoes

each year, and each one is decorated differently," says Debra. "But we always place the largest tree in the entry, because this is the room with the tallest ceiling, due to the exterior's turret."

The entry tree, as the first display of Christmas witnessed in the home, is lavishly decorated with antique ornaments and white poinsettias. "We use old china and gold in the entry, making it by far the most formal Christmas space," she says.

In contrast, the Christmas tree in the den is pure whimsy and fun, decorated entirely with toys. "We use big, funny old lights, and it's very funky," says Debra.

Besides trimming a multitude of trees, the family also decorates each of the home's five fireplaces with natural greens and wraps the staircase in sweet-smelling garlands of fir. Outside, improvements added to the house by the Joneses, including picket fences and multi-level decks, come alive beneath strand after strand of tiny white lights, making the home a glittering jewel in the canyons during the holiday season.

Woven into each holiday's decor is that year's find of Christmas

# Yuletide Echoes

**Right:** *Opening*

*onto the*

*kitchen, the*

*family room*

*hosts a plethora*

*of informal*

*meals during*

*the holidays,*

*when the*

*Joneses*

*entertain often.*

**Below:** *All five*

*fireplaces bear*

*holiday greens.*

✳

collectibles from flea markets and tag sales, which Debra faithfully scours all year long. Last year, the find was antique soldiers, which were incorporated into the home's outdoor decorations. "Every year, there's something new. But somehow, the house still manages to look calm," says Debra.

Somehow, too, the home retains a serene, unified character year-round, even though it's filled with Debra's odds-and-ends assemblage of collectibles of various styles, periods, themes, and moods. "I've been eclectic all of my life, since I was a kid," Debra says.

"For me, there doesn't have to be a set structure to designing a home. I'm hooked on collecting, and the result is a very hodge-podge look—everything from traditional to Oriental to contemporary. I don't design for look but for comfort."

That's one reason her decorating

**Opposite:**

*Whitewashed cedar walls and strategically placed folk art, plus fun pieces such as the antique rooster-turned-lamp, preserve a light mood in the living room.*

**Above left:** *Debra has an unerring eye for arranging unrelated items and for pulling together fabrics, shapes, and textures,* **left.**

✳

style is under the banner of country design. "I want a home to be warm and cozy—not such a statement."

Apparently a lot of other folks agree. Although she doesn't bill herself as a professional designer, Debra often is called upon to render decorating aid, especially now that she owns and runs her late father's home construction business.

Nostalgia is another reason Debra's eclecticism has a country feel. "I had a great childhood with a lot of happy memories," she says. "So, whenever I go to flea markets, I try to find things that remind me of those memories—things like some glassware I remember from my grandmother's house. What I end up with are fun things that maybe are a little eccentric."

Unlike some collectors, Debra doesn't believe in retiring some of her collectibles to make room for newer acquisitions. Hers is an ongoing, ever-growing process. "Our home is a matter of years and years of collecting all of the stuff we buy on the weekends, then finding a place to put it," she says.

When Debra likes something, she says she uses it "whether it really goes with anything or not." The red and white swag curtains in the living room and entry are a case in point. She says, "I took these with us from our last house because I really like them, and I just made them work here, even though the fabrics don't actually match anything else in the rooms.

"I make a lot of mistakes, but I'm just not afraid. You can have a chair that's a little off, but after a while, it all comes together."

That kind of confidence comes from growing up in a family oriented around the home construction business. "When you're not only around interiors but also the structure of the house," Debra says, "you can decide in the morning that you want a window cut and have it done by the afternoon. You

## Yuletide Echoes

*Right: Warm wood paneling, a blazing fire, and a tree trimmed with toys make the den inviting for Shannon and Tangeray and the family's holiday visitors.*

*Below: These nutcrackers preside over the merriment.*

can anticipate the results of change and not worry as much."

She even goes as far as saying she enjoys a house that's not quite finished. "It doesn't bother me to have the whole end of the house torn off. I would rather have the house in turmoil, because it means that I'm getting to do something new that I wanted," she says.

When she and Parker bought their house from her mother five years ago, they immediately changed it. "It had been a 1950s Chinese-Hawaiian California track home," says Debra. "My mother removed the roof rafters with the flared ends and the Chinese red doors, added a second story, and gave it a real lodge look. We took that rustic feel and softened it, painting everything."

Now, surrounded with treasures—from 1930s figurines to antique fish posters and vintage fabrics everywhere—Debra, Parker, and Shannon prepare for the holidays and generously share the results of their labors. Each year, they host a formal dinner for the entire family.

And, with loved ones all gathered, out across the canyons echo the joyous sounds of a family celebrating Christmas with love. ■

# Index

Have *Country Home*® magazine delivered to your door. For information, write to: Mr. Robert Austin, P.O. Box 10667, Des Moines, IA 50336-0667. Or call toll-free 1-800-678-2666.